WHEN THINGS HAPPEN TO PEOPLE:

The Field Beyond Good and Bad

WHEN THINGS HAPPEN TO PEOPLE:

The Field Beyond Good and Bad

by S. Elise Peeples

Eshu House

Publishing
Berkeley, CA

Eshu House

Publishing
Berkeley, CA

Cover painting by Peggy Ho, (see www.PeggyHo.com); photographed by Frances Hartwell.

Cover designed by Elise Peeples and Peggy Ho.

Poem appearing in Chapter Five, "Someday I'll be Grateful" by Karen Jandorf previously appeared in *A Healing Journey: Writing Together Through Breast Cancer*, Sharon Bray, Ed.D., Amherst Writers & Artists Press, 2004. Printed with permission from Karen Jandorf.

Library of Congress Control Number: 2011920149

ISBN: 978-0-9656576-4-8

To Elenna Rubin Goodman and the Bay Area Daré for their un-flagging support of my journey, for reminding me every step of the way to reside in a wider awareness than just my small self, and to pay attention to and nurture the healing field that includes so much more than any singular self. Thank you for participating in this powerful personal and community initiation.

AND

To Adam David Miller, my husband. Thank you for teaching me about the speed of love.

ACKNOWLEDGEMENTS

I thank all, both seen and unseen: family, Daré members, friends, ancestors, and strangers who were involved in some way in creating the healing field that held me throughout this ordeal. Thanks to all those who were on the e-mail list: Alan, Alexis, Betsy, Bola, Brenda, Brigid, Bruce, Constance, Cress, Cynthia, Deena, Donna, Dipti, Elenna, Gael, Gail, Garner, Gloria, Jane, Jim, Joan, Joya, Joyce, Juli, Karen, Katie, Ken and Linda, Lacey, Laura, Linda, Liz, Lucy C, Lucy D, Malcolm, Marilyn, Mark, Marti, Meg, Nicki, OwlSnake, Pamela, Peg, Pemba, Phil, Ruth, Sarah, Saundra, Siddika, Susana, Suzie, Viviane, and Yolanda.

I thank my grandmother, Harriet, for the role she played from the other side in helping to identify the tumor in good time.

Thank you to Pemba Pierini, Adam David Miller, and Elenna Rubin Goodman who read drafts and gave me feedback.

A special thanks to Peggy Ho (and to her consultant, Julia Montrond) who painted a picture of my altar for the cover of this book, and consulted with me in the design of the cover.

Thanks to Deena Metzger, Dipti, Mogera Anderson and Karen Jandorf who, having been through breast cancer and mastectomy themselves, helped me so much as I entered this unknown territory.

Thanks to Joyce Jenkins, copyeditor, for her patience, diligence, and commitment. Her careful engagement improved this book considerably. (See more of her work at www.PoetryFlash.org.)

Thanks to Lucy Colvin on many levels, but especially her engineering of the plaster cast, the centerpiece of my altar and pictured on the cover of this book. Thanks to the owners of the other forty assisting fingers: Elenna, Dipti, Nicki, and Pamela.

Thanks to Alan Wick, Alexis Lavine, Elenna Rubin Goodman, Yolanda Vazquez, Viviane De Leon Bias, Owlsnake, Lucy Colvin, and Joan Marie Passalacqua who gave me one-on-one sound healing or bodywork.

For their continuing support, thanks to my mother Ruth, sister Sue, and my brothers, Jim and Mark, and wives, Ann and Becky.

For generously offering a writing refuges, I thank Nicole Milner and Sue Peeples.

Thanks to all of the members of the Sound, Voice, and Music Healing program at the California Institute of Integral Studies in San Francisco, especially Kaaren, Maria G, Maria L, Lucinda, Phyllis, Tina, and Beth for helping me thrive in my new life. And to Silvia Nakkach, the director of the program, for having the vision of a sound healing certificate program and for creating a fabulous curriculum.

I am so thankful to have had health coverage through this ordeal. Thank you to Dr. Veronica Shim and to Kaiser Permanente Medical Center in Oakland and its staff for the detection and treatment of the tumor. Thank you to Sue Edelstein, my physical therapist, who helped me with my injured shoulder and gave me moral support. May this country soon establish universal health care so that human suffering is not compounded by financial worry.

Thank you to the dreams, intuitions, ancestors, nature spirits— of land, and sea (especially at Steep Ravine), of other-than-human beings, the seen and the unseen teachers along the way.

Table of Contents

Für Elise II/Full Moon

"There is a grove darkened with leafy oak and pine;
the rays of the sun are barely allowed to creep in."
— Ovid

The full moon is a perfect gold nipple,
settling far on the Western horizon,
ritual bearing of death and regeneration.

In the fourth millennium, fingers formed
bare chests on living goddesses of Malta.
Just now, a crow flies over the vision.

It is the hardest thought:
contemplate this empty female curve.
Your weapons wax and wane - tides.

The promise—replace mothering so
something will grow in place
of your lost breast – pain also promise.

Invoke Artemis, Amazos, breastless
mothers removed a breast from each newborn girl.
Interference was not allowed with such quests.

It is the time of Warrior Motherline.
Call your weapons   your music   your prowess,
Moon moves out from her shroud now.

Tonight the full moon is a perfect gold nipple.
Setting far in a dark Western sky.
Warrior woman rebirths her own quest.

—Meg Withers

August 6, 2009

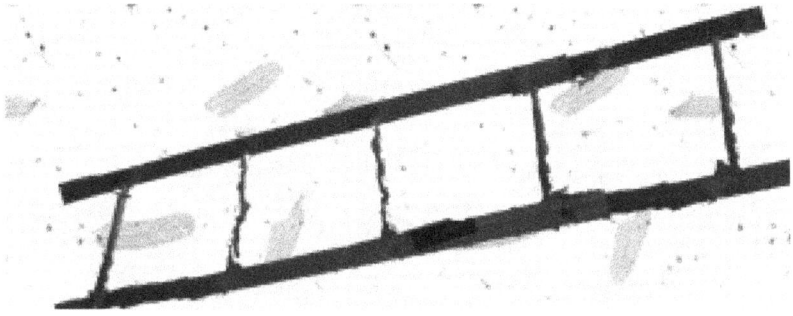

INTRODUCTION

I began this book because of a series of e-mails I sent and that were sent in reply to me before and after I had a mastectomy on September 4, 2009. My original intent was simply to publish e-mails that had meant so much to me. However, when I started putting them together, I realized that the story I wanted to tell required a recounting of the context as well; the story enlarged itself to include details that I considered to be relevant to the whole journey.

In hindsight, I can see that what I was doing throughout this ordeal was to attempt to change the focus of my attention from what is "me" and "mine" to a wider awareness of peace-making and healing, not just in my life, but in my communities and beyond.

I compare this change of focus to a film I once saw called Cosmic Voyage[1] where the lens of the camera looked at reality from different distances. First, it zoomed in to the microscopic level, and then it zoomed out, in stages, all the way to outer space. At the microscopic level, atoms looked

---

1   Cosmic Voyage is a 1996 short documentary produced in the IMAX format, directed by Bayley Silleck, produced by Jeffrey Marvin, and narrated by Morgan Freeman.

chaotic until the camera zoomed out a little, and the pattern became clear. Then it would zoom a little further out and everything looked chaotic for a while until it zoomed out far enough to allow the viewer to once again recognize patterns.

You will see that at one point in the story I was asked if I could be the vehicle for a miracle for the community, and I answered, yes. To me, a miracle occurs when we can let go of judgment, cause and effect, reward and punishment—in fact, all dualisms—and keep the focus spacious, allowing for a glimpse into a different level of reality where miracles happen. With this different focus, events and what seem like isolated incidents and individuals show themselves to be deeply connected, forming a new sort of pattern.

Seeing or sensing that other level of reality, however, required that I disengage from the details of my daily life long enough to experience chaos and "not knowing." Things occurred on this journey that are unexplainable in this day-to-day reality but which made intuitive sense when I zoomed out. These glimpses into a larger reality came in the form of synchronicities, dreams, messages from ancestors or animals, lessons from unlikely sources, and intuitions that I could not attribute to any likely source.

This account is not meant to be a "how-to" for people going through a similar surgery; that would be impossible to extrapolate from my limited experience, as each person going through something like this is in a totally different circumstance.

But this book *is* an attempt to document my journey in which I held, in whatever ways possible, an attitude of receptivity and openness to guidance from both the seen and unseen.

If I learned nothing else, I learned that one can only "know" the next step, not the ones that will follow. Projecting oneself into the future, planning all the next steps, dissipates the energy that is needed to clearly ascertain and take each step as it is given.

I admit that if you had told me a year ago that I would be writing about such a private surgery and that I would have involved just about everyone I know and then some, I would have said that you were out of your mind. I tend to be one who suffers alone and quietly. But for some reason this ordeal became public before it had time to be closely held, and then it was off and running. I had a community. I had an e-mail list of over fifty people. And, as you will see, this community was intimately involved the whole way through.

THE LADDER

The beginning of the story seems to be a day in February of 2009 when I drove to Santa Cruz via Highway 880 with Elenna Rubin Goodman, founder of the Bay Area Daré, (Shona word for Council), a healing and peace-making circle of which I have been a member for eight years.[2]

---

2   Daré is a sacred community gathering which places healing, community, peace building and the restoration of our world at its center. Daré came to the Bay Area through a collaboration between Zimbabwean traditional healer Mandaza Kandemwa, Deena Metzger, and Elenna Rubin Goodman. See BayAreaDare.com for more information.

While we were driving in the fast lane going up a hill, I was recounting to Elenna a dream I had had about a didgeridoo.[3] Suddenly, a ladder that had come loose from a pick-up truck landed broadside across our lane. I swerved to the right around the edge of it, into the next lane, and then swerved back again into our lane.

That sounds all well and good—no one was badly injured and the car was fine. Except that I remain convinced that there was no way in this day-to-day reality for us to have missed the ladder, considering how fast we were traveling in one direction, and how the ladder was bouncing along in the other. Time seemed to stop to give us a chance to get out of the ladder's way.

We entered into an alternative reality that day; a miracle happened.

For twenty-four hours after the ladder descended, I was fine. Then I started having flashbacks, seeing both of us in the hospital or dead. I seemed to be experiencing post traumatic stress. I remember making offerings to the land and any Spirits that might have been involved in keeping us alive. I just remember thinking that I was indebted to something somewhere.

The next day I developed cellulitis in my right foot, a serious condition that has twice required that I be hospitalized and placed on intravenous antibiotics. This time, I was given oral antibiotic and told to keep my toes above my nose for a while and to stay in that position except to

---

3   A didgeridoo is an ancient Australian wind instrument that is essentially a hollow tube. I have been playing the didgeridoo for about five years and use it mostly for meditation and healing work.

eat and go to the bathroom. Determined not to end up in the hospital again, I followed doctor's orders.   I also saw an acupuncturist who said that the near-miss with the ladder could have caused the toxins in my foot to come to a head.

A few days later OwlSnake[4], a shaman friend of mine who sees spirits, particularly ancestors, came to my house (so I could keep my toes elevated) to tell me of a vision she'd had in which I was one of seven people who had spiritual work to do that was in some way blocked. Her job was to help unblock the energy. We talked for a while and couldn't figure out where I was blocked. I had been following the path of didgeridoo player and healer with no blocks, going through every door that presented itself. So what could it be?

I casually mentioned that I had two novels in the drawer that had been there a while. She asked what they were about, and I responded that they were both about voices from the dead. She perked up and asked more. When I told her that one of the manuscripts, *Strands*, was written to fulfill a promise to my no-longer-living grandmother Harriet, and the other was about death and the ancestors, she immediately insisted that this was where the block was. I needed to publish the story without delay. That counsel seemed right, and yet I still did nothing but think about it. I considered calling someone I knew of who might help me find a way to get it published, but I did not call that person.

One thing I did decide then was to enroll in a sound

---

healing class to better understand what I was doing with the didgeridoo. I was drawn to enroll in the Sound, Voice, and Music certificate program that was to start at the California Institute of Integral Studies[5] in September.

A couple days after I made that decision, I had an accident. This time the accident occurred very much in day-to-day reality as I fell into a yard waste bin, badly injuring my right arm and shoulder—nothing broken but my ligaments were stretched beyond reckoning.

I did not connect this fall to anything but clumsiness until a month later when I started physical therapy and felt a piercing pain under my right arm. While investigating the cause of that pain, I found a lump the size of a golf ball in my right breast. It couldn't have been there long—it was just too big to be ignored.

Grandmother
Harriet

_____

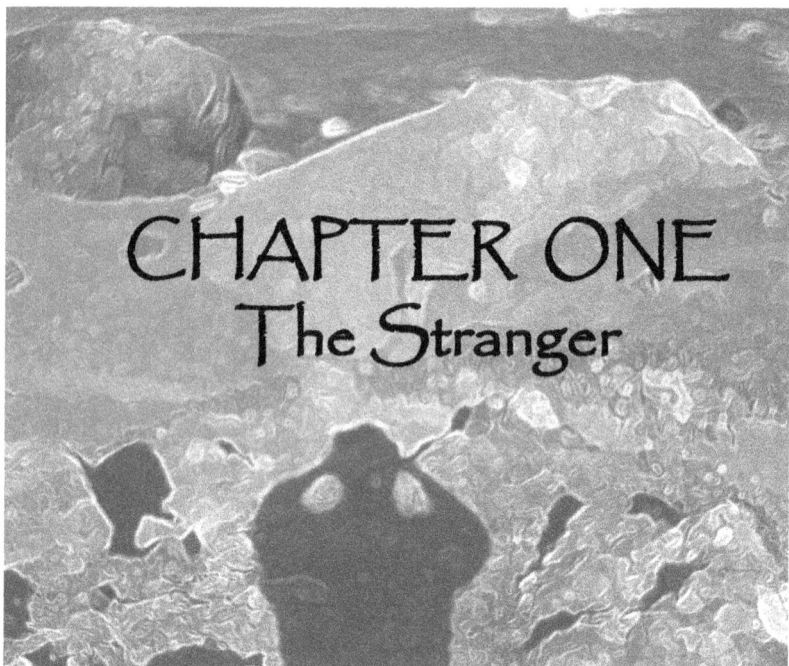

CHAPTER ONE
The Stranger

For one long day I kept the lump to myself, hoping it was just my imagination and that it would go away on its own. The next day, Saturday, seeing that the growth was still there, I called Kaiser and made an appointment to see an Ob-Gyn doctor on Monday. Then I called Elenna to talk to her about a concert we were to attend that evening and at some point in the conversation, I burst into tears. After I told her what was going on, she kicked right into gear offering to schedule a music Daré on my behalf the next night. I resisted at first, thinking it would be impossible to get people together on such short notice, and worried that we might be making a big deal out of nothing.

MUSIC DARÉ

May 16

Dear Daré Companions,

There will be a Music Daré for Elise Pee-
ples this Sunday evening, May 17th at 7:30
PM. If it is at all possible, please come.

Elise learned yesterday that she has a
lump in her right breast. She will be seeing
a Kaiser physician on Monday morning.
The period before a name or diagnosis is
attached to a condition is a very fluid and
potent time to offer healing, balancing en-
ergies. We will gather on the eve of Elise's ap-
pointment to offer ourselves as a container
into which the mystery of healing can enter,
support the restoration of balance among
all of her cells and to call into their natu-
ral and healthy state the cells that have iso-
lated themselves into a distinct mass within
her breast.

Please bring the instruments, sacred ob-
jects and offerings that you feel will support
us in being present for and with Elise. We
will gather at 7:30 and begin as close to
7:45 as we can.

With blessings and gratitude for having
a community such as this to call upon in a
moment such as this... elenna

∾

For a music Daré, the community (both experienced Daré folk and others who are there because they are close to the one for whom the Daré is called) gathers to support the person's healing in whatever ways are possible through music and energy work. The person on whom the group focuses prepares through prayer and offering herself as a vehicle for healing on many levels. She discerns relevant information about the dis-ease and her own prayers for healing that she would like the group to support.

The first music Daré we ever held was for a woman who had breast cancer. She had done everything that was asked of her, including radiation and chemo, and still she had to have a mastectomy. When she went into the surgery, Elenna talked to the surgeon and told her that she would like her to be not just a surgeon but a healer, and that this woman was giving her breast as an offering to go on living. That music Daré, which I attended, was very powerful. Afterwards, two owls showed up in the trees across the street, a sight that had never before been witnessed in those trees.

I went into this music Daré saying that maybe we would be there for half an hour since I was pretty sure this was unnecessary, and that I would be fine. But the session lasted two hours. We called Spirit[1] with music, and I joined in playing my didgeridoo.

When I was asked to tell the story of this illness, I remember saying that an uninvited stranger had shown

---

1   In virtually every culture, human beings have used toning, chanting, drumming and singing to praise their Creator and to heal their bodies and spirits. During Calling to Spirit we create sound to acknowledge each other, to listen broadly and deeply, and to call ourselves present to the Spirit, the Ancestors and the community.
There are many ways to participate in the Calling of Spirit, whether one participates through rhythm, singing, or meditation. In Daré we encourage sound to emerge out of stillness, to invite in what is asking to be heard here and now, rather than performing prepared or rehearsed pieces. We collaborate with each other in an improvisational and continuous call and response: to ourselves, to each other, and to Spirit. In so doing, we become a community of sacred instruments that allow healing vibrations to manifest.

up in my breast and I wasn't sure why. It felt like a kind of fiction where the story begins when a stranger comes to town. Subsequently this stranger affects everyone in different ways; therein lies the story (and the moral of the story).

I lay in the middle of the room, surrounded by love and music in many forms including drums, didgeridoo, voice, rattles, rain stick, bells. I felt supported and loved. Not having to face the next steps alone made all the difference in the way I could walk through it. Three women offered to come the next day and be there for the appointment.

A STEP DOWN THE MEDICAL ROAD

Before the appointment, I met Elenna at a café. While waiting, I took out an e-mail I had gotten that morning from a Daré member who had been at the healing session the night before. She'd had a vision in which she needed to make an exchange for the healing that had been offered, and she described what had been called for in great detail. I read it to Elenna and then realized that I had printed it on the back of a draft page of my novel, *Strands*. I read the draft page and found that it, too, referred to an exchange, one that happened in the book to the main character, Emma, who is based on my mother. The ocean had unexpectedly come up over her foot, and she wondered if she needed to give something back for that gift she had received. I began to think about what it was I needed to give in exchange. And for what? For going on living?

Two other women friends met me at the appointment, and again I felt the support of the community. Maybe it was to the community I needed to give back?

I wanted to have the biopsy as soon as possible so we thought of scheduling another music Daré, this time mostly with didgeridoos, for that Wednesday evening. (I was teaching didgeridoo to a number of Daré members at that time.) Yolanda[2] offered to have the gathering at her place.

I finally e-mailed the woman who I thought could help me publish the novel. As soon as I pushed the send button, I got a call from Kaiser saying that the biopsy had been scheduled for Thursday morning. I took note of the "coincidence."

ॐ

May 19
Dear friends,

I have an appointment for the next step in my diagnostic process at 9:30 Thursday morning. So the Wednesday healing session at Yolanda's is at a perfect time.

Please bring your didge if you have one and if you don't, feel free to bring another instrument, use your voice, or hold space.

Thank you to everyone who has been holding me in their prayers—I appreciate it and know I am being held.

Love,
Elise

ॐ

---

2   Yolanda (Pritam Hari Kaur) is a certified Iyengar teacher devoted to yoga for thirty-eight years, and a Nationally Certified bodyworker with advanced training in CranioSacral Therapy, brain and spinal cord restrictions, and autonomic nervous system balance. See www.quietmind.com.

May 21
Dear ones,

The news is that the lump is not a cyst and therefore cannot be drained and sent home. It is a mass and has to be biopsied. We tried that today but unfortunately they did not get enough mass to make a diagnosis and I have to go back in tomorrow for a more invasive biopsy. The mass is not a usual one and thus the mistake about which biopsy would be best. So in limbo land we remain. It is possible that they will have results before the end of the day tomorrow but I am not certain of this.

Thank you again to all those who came last night to Yolanda's for the didge and energy heal-a-thon. It was certainly gratifying to me as a teacher to be ministered to by all those didges (and, of course, didge players!). Not to mention the rest of the energy work that was given to me. I feel so blessed to be part of this community!

❧

Elenna came with me to the biopsy and after waiting for at least forty-five minutes, a woman and her assistant came rushing in. She lunged straight for my breast and said, "Oh, it looks like cancer!" Then she proceeded to set up for the biopsy and to conduct it. Sometime during that process, she said, "It's not behaving like cancer—no, I don't think it is, but we won't know until the biopsy comes back." She threw around a few other medical words that I didn't know, while pushing and shoving roughly against my breast.

I finally asked her who she was; she was taken aback. She looked accusingly at her assistant as if *she* should have introduced her. After she told me her name, I was reassured because she had been recommended by a good friend of mine. Still, the whole experience of the biopsy had been disconcerting.

❧

May 22
Dear everyone,
        Thanks so much for holding me in your prayers. I just re-
turned from a long day at Kaiser and had another biopsy, mammo-
gram and ultrasound. The surgeon does not believe this is behaving
like cancer but more like a collection of fat cells. We can't know for
sure (as sure as they get) until we get biopsy results which won't be
available until Tuesday or Wednesday. Until then, may we continue to
hold a positive thought.
        Love to you all,
        Elise

RETREAT AT MT. SHASTA

That weekend I attended a retreat led by OwlSnake (shaman and medicine woman) held in the shadow of Mount Shasta. I drove up in a car with three other women from Daré. I was in a state of suspension, not knowing the results of the latest biopsy. The work we were to do was with the ancestors and I was ready to talk to mine, especially my grandmother Harriet. I knew that I had let her down by not yet publishing the novel; yet I was so preoccupied with "the stranger" that I didn't have much energy for the book.

At one point in the retreat, I met with OwlSnake privately, and we discussed my writing projects. I still wasn't sure which novel to focus on publishing since I had two almost ready to go. She advised me then to get *Strands* published right away to carry out my promise to Harriet.

On Sunday I woke up and shared a story with my tentmate about Harriet. When she was in her early nineties she had told me a story of how one day, thousands of butterflies appeared on her porch. This story had felt more like a dream than a linear conversation and I interpreted it as such, knowing that butterflies were the symbol of feminism in those days.

Later that morning, we conducted a ceremony by immersing ourselves in a lake. Just after I came up out of the water, a butterfly flew by. Because of the way everyone was facing, I was the only one who saw it.

On the way home, we got spring water where the Sacramento River begins. That seemed important to me as a kind of cleansing. We talked about the tumor and my novel. It seemed more and more clear that there was a connection, though no one could articulate exactly what it was. We spoke of it being on the right side, the masculine side, and what a stranger in a breast might mean.

BIOPSIES CONTINUED

May 27
Dear all,

I just received news that the biopsy showed no cancer. But just so I couldn't get excited and feel fine, the doctor said I am still not in the clear because there is so much of a mass there and the biopsy could have missed something. She wants to check again and is going out of town for the next ten days.

So I will let everyone know when the next appointment is scheduled and I ask that you continue to hold me in your prayers. Thanks so much for all of your support.
     Love,
     Elise

❧

Dear all,

The next appointment with the doctor is Tuesday, June 9 at 1:45. She will be continuing the investigation of what this stranger/lump is. Thanks so much for all of your continued prayers and support.

Love,

Elise

❧

For the biopsy on June 9, the doctor was maybe an hour late. Another Daré friend, Pamela, was with me; we talked quietly while we waited. When the doctor finally came in, she paused a minute, looked around, and said, "It feels peaceful in here." We talked about peace for a few seconds, and then she was back in rush-mode. She took a number of samples from different parts of the tumor but was still puzzled about what this was.

VEHICLE FOR A MIRACLE

One weekend, Deena Metzger came to Oakland to lead a workshop with our Daré. She, along with her husband Michael Ortiz Hill, had brought the Daré from Zimbabwe to the United States. A healer and writer, she had written *Tree,* a book about her own experiences with breast cancer thirty-some years ago. I met privately with her before the workshop, and we talked about what message this tumor was bringing. I shared with her the metaphor of the stranger. She asked how I wanted to respond to the stranger. I said that on a bad day I just wanted him/her to go away and leave me alone. But I thought that perhaps the stranger was bringing a gift that I was not able to understand at this point. Still, my thinking had not progressed beyond listening to the stranger and then politely asking him to leave. I wanted the tumor shrunk and gone.

Deena suggested to me that I entertain the notion that I was being asked to be a vehicle for a miracle for the community.

Later in the workshop, when each of us identified our gifts to the community, I said with as much conviction as I could muster that my gift was to offer myself as a vehicle for a miracle for the community.

PILGRIMAGE TO THE SEA

After the workshop, I was scheduled to go on retreat to Steep Ravine, a state park with cabins at the ocean, north of San Francisco. At least twice a year for over ten years I have been going to Steep Ravine. It is a second home to me.

The cabins are so popular that they must be reserved six-seven months in advance so it was serendipitous that I had planned so many months before to be there at this momentous time. I agreed with Deena's suggestion that I devote a day while I was there to pray and work with the didgeridoo on the tumor if that seemed appropriate.

❧

June 13

Dear all,
The last biopsy also showed negative for cancer. However, the doctor cannot say what it is and wants to take it out. The smaller it is,

if and when that happens, the better for the body.

I am asking for your help in creating a miracle through prayer and vibration to shrink this to nothing before I am scheduled for surgery (either June 23rd or in August sometime).

I am asking for prayers particularly between 8 am and 4 pm on Monday June 15th as I will be at Steep Ravine (the ocean) in consultation with Spirit during those hours asking for help in shrinking and re-integrating the tumor and working with my self-healing didge if that is called for.

I will certainly let you know when and if surgery is scheduled. Thanks so much for all of your continued prayers and support.

Love,
Elise

∾

On June 14, I arrived at Steep Ravine with my friend Peg. That night I had a dream: *I am at a concert that goes until dawn. Afterwards, people are buying food at the Safeway near Ocean Beach in San Francisco but I don't because I am fasting. Someone asks me how I knew the concert would be good. And I can't say, but I just knew. I am to go into silence for the day but others around me speak and take out didgeridoos to begin playing. A Daré member is there and she begins playing but the instrument sounds like an oboe instead of a didgeridoo.*

I was struck by the dream and now felt an impetus to fast for the day which I hadn't planned. And the "coincidence" of the oboe... I had a dream a number of years ago when I was working on the second draft of *Strands*. In the dream *I am handed an oboe and told that it will be my instrument. I protest that I don't know how to play it and can only play the flute. The man just shrugs and walks away.*

I remember the dream so clearly because it portrayed how I felt writing the novel, as if I had no idea how to write fiction but could only write non-fiction. And yet I was being asked to proceed.

That day at Steep Ravine, I took my didgeridoo, drinking water, and the manuscript of *Strands* and went off by myself to fast and pray. I found a private place leaning against a huge rock where I was out of the wind but could hear the ocean beating against the rocks and see the pelicans rounding the corner on fishing forays.

I began by praying about whether I should use the didgeridoo to attempt to shrink the tumor. The worry was that should it be cancer, I would not want to visualize the tumor dissolving since then it could go into the blood stream. I asked for guidance, and when I opened my eyes there was a lady bug on the didge. I decided that meant it was okay to use the didge. I did this intuitively after prayer, but later, when I had access to the Internet, I found out that lady bugs are said to be dedicated to the Virgin Mary, a figure who arises a number of times in my novel. Also, they are said to be related to spiritual devotion and letting go of fears and worries. It is said that if the lady bug lands on you when you are sick, when it flies away, it will take the sickness with it.

I called the directions in the Siberian way which I use in my daily practice, calling first East (direction of earth, golden, peace), then North (air, green, health, prosperity, well-being), West (fire, red, the great mystery), South (water, dark blue, the internal warrior of discernment), and All Directions (space, moonlight white, unconditional love).

As I visualized the lump shrinking, I sang, "The earth, the air, the fire, the water, return, return, return, return.... I thought: the stranger is made of elements and I am asking that they return to where they belong. Of course, then I must also return to where I belong, in my lineage, connected to my ancestors, and to all that is and all that will be. I wrote in my journal: "I must return from forgetfulness, the disease of our culture... rampant, contagious, destructive."

Later, in meditation, I got an image of baring my breast on the lichen-covered rock, and I did that. Reminded of a scene in the novel, I opened the manuscript to about where I thought the scene was located and instead opened to a passage I had completely forgotten was in the book. Emma, the main character, has just finished a conversation with the ghost of her mother who had been committed to a mental institution for thirty-seven years, and says:

> "Good night mother," I say calling her mother for the first time ever. Saying it makes tears spring to my eyes; I brush them away. No use crying over spilt milk. An image leaps to my mind– a breast slashed open and spilling milk out all over that medieval institution. I stay with the image until it becomes an ocean of milk flooding the place, closing it down."

Just then the sun emerged from the clouds for a brief moment, and I bared my right breast to it and to the wind. Such a vulnerable small thing my breast was. Such a vulnerable small thing I was.

The wind and chill picked up again so I rearranged myself to stay warm.

Throughout the day, I alternated silence with didge playing. At 3:30 the following came to me as I got a strange sense of what was real. I wrote in my journal: "I guess I never believed it—that voices came to me on the wind and the rain. I believed I wrote a fictional account in which the heroine hears these voices. I never took it seriously enough—never truly owned these ancestors as mine. I am feeling it now—the wake up—the reality, the belief. Faith in what has gone before will heal the world. The cutting apart of worlds, this one and that, *that* is the ignorance that brings false bliss. I am converted now, after this day of prayer, I believe. I am not now half-hearted, not hedging, not holding back. Thank you, Grandmother. Thank you spirits of the East, North, West, South, and Space. Thank you wind, sun, water, earth. I have returned."

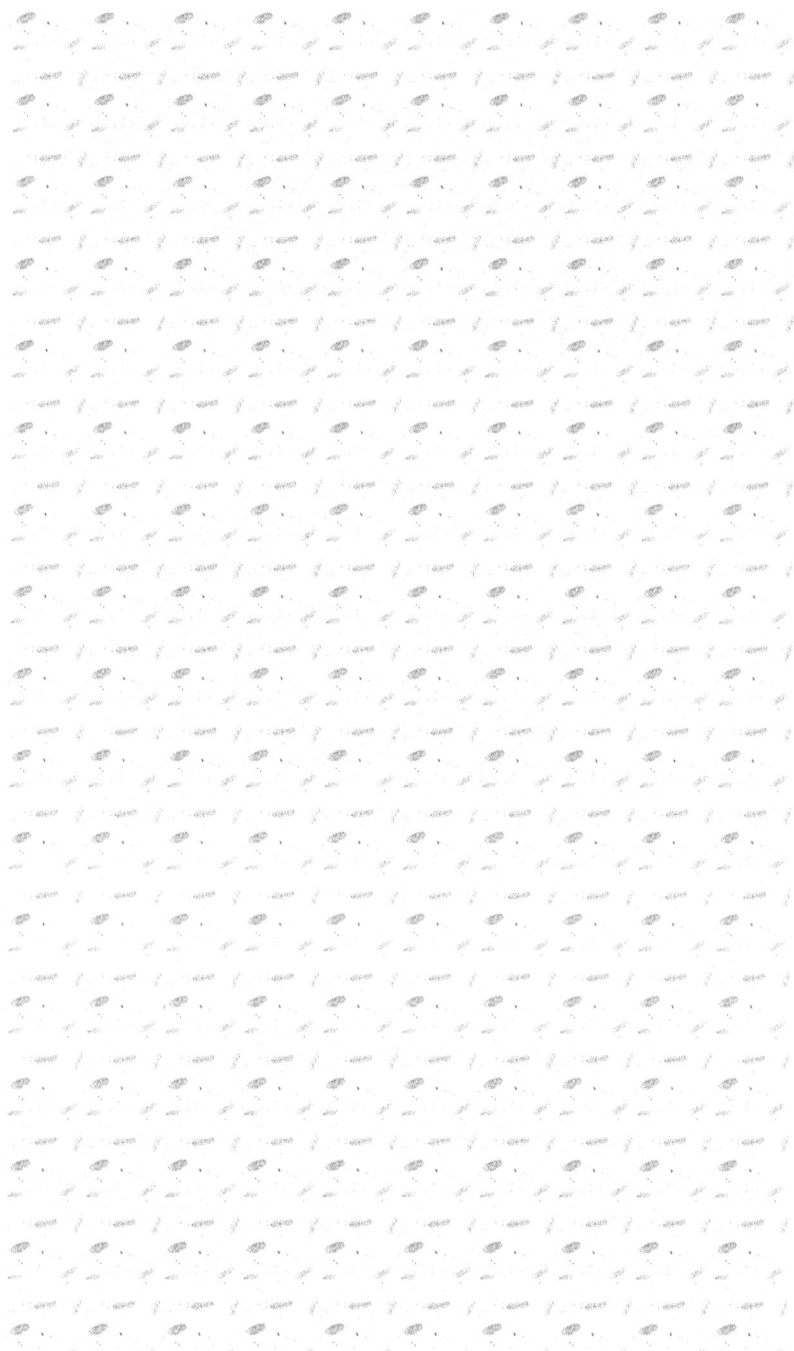

CHAPTER TWO
Who is that Stranger?

(And why didn't he take his stuff with him when he left?)

When I returned from Steep Ravine, I found out that the lumpectomy had been scheduled for June 23, less than a week away. I was ready for the stranger to be gone, as it was hurting and seemed to be aggravating everything. Because my arm was still quite injured, I was in physical therapy on a regular basis.

The surgery was done at Kaiser Richmond as an outpatient procedure. Elenna insisted to the surgeon that she be allowed to be in the room and, though it was against policy, they finally agreed to let her stay. We were aiming at creating a field of healing, and since I was to be under a local anesthesia and a sedative, it was helpful to have Elenna in the room, attentively witnessing and praying.

I have mentioned how hurried my surgeon always seemed to be. Well, on this day, she did not wait for the local to take effect before she made the cut. I felt the knife go in. Because of the sedative, I didn't scream out but it wasn't at all pleasant. The anesthesiologist saw my distress and I thought passed along the information to the surgeon. Then it was over. The tumor was substantial, large and yellow.

The surgeon still didn't know what it was. She reported that she had had to cut off roots to get the thing out. I was fairly certain that this would be the end of it and that I could go on with my life.

I waited again for more than a week, and then went in to see the doctor on July 1. Because I was so sure it would be good news, I didn't take anyone with me this time. But the lab report advocated another surgery.

The tumor was called a Phyllodes tumor, and the report said it was neither benign nor malignant but somewhere in between. The doctor explained that this kind of tumor is very rare (one percent of all breast cancers) but that it is particularly dangerous if any of it is left inside because this kind of tumor could metastasize not in the breast, necessarily, but directly into the bloodstream, showing up in a major organ. She recommended another surgery to take out the margins around the tumor and the roots. There would be no way to check to make sure they got it all as what we were talking about at this point was microscopic. I could pursue alternative healing methods but there would be no way to verify whether they did or did not work.

As she left, she looked over her shoulder and said, "Yes, I don't think I would recommend a mastectomy." And then she was out the door, leaving me devastated and wondering why on earth she would even consider a mastectomy, why I even had to hear that word. I left the place crying, doubting that I would agree to the surgery the doctor had recommended—I had a very bad feeling about it.

I faxed the lab report to a friend who works in a breast cancer unit at a different major hospital in the Bay Area and she showed it to her most trusted doctor. She called me right before I left again for Steep Ravine. I was stunned by the recommendation of her doctor, who said if it were she and she were small-breasted, she would have a mastectomy. She went on to say that in a lumpectomy, if the surgeon doesn't get all the margins, there would be a risk of the tumor metastasizing; I would have to have a mammogram every three months for the rest of my life.

I didn't even tell my husband this news since I was just about to leave town and didn't have time to discuss it. I got in the car with my friend Meg who was to be with me at Steep Ravine, confused and disbelieving—how could someone say that I should have a mastectomy when I didn't even have cancer? It was simply unbelievable.

Again, serendipitously, I had scheduled time away at my second home, a place where I feel close to the elements, to the whisper of wisdom from the sea, to pure grace.

DECISIONS MUST BE MADE

That weekend, the Fourth of July, I vacillated between absolute dread of a mastectomy to the dread of a second operation in which they did not get all of the tumor out, thus requiring a mastectomy anyway. I had a strong feeling that even if we did another surgery to get the margins, they would not be sure—the roots after all, would involve a lot more tissue.

In my own psyche, I had glimmers of what it meant to make sure the roots were gone. What I might have to become, to change the very roots of my way of operating in the world? It was not a thought I entertained with calm and curiosity. I was terrified, especially of the unknown place I was entering.

I had sleepless nights of not knowing. Meg was matter-of-fact with me and was supportive but not intrusive. I thought at first that a mastectomy was an extreme option, a violent option for something which just had potential and not any reality at the moment. I compared it to calling someone a terrorist if they had just *thought* of blowing something up but had done nothing. So we blow up their house. It seemed like such an overreaction.

The last night I was there, after Meg had left and my husband Adam had arrived, I awoke at about 3 a.m. I wandered outside and the almost-full moon was shining very bright. For a while, I took in the moonlight through the back of my neck, facing the mountain. The image of mountaintop removal came to me suddenly and made me sob. That's what this felt like, mountaintop removal. I could not see how having a mastectomy fit with being a peacemaker. If I stood for non-violence and peace, how could I do this violence to my own body? It was important to my rational mind to figure this out.

Then I turned and faced the moon and bared my breast. I prayed; I begged; I cried. I was torn in half and could get no sleep. Adam got up and went outside to use the rest room and when he came back in I talked to him. He hummed me a lullaby and then went back to bed. I still didn't sleep but watched the moon set, becoming a deep orange and then disappearing slowly into the ocean.

I came home in that condition and stayed that way for a while. I called my sister who is a nurse practitioner. I faxed her the lab report; she researched the tumor and found a doctor on the East Coast who has had more contact with this kind of tumor than anyone else, but that turned into a dead end. When I told her I had a bad feeling about the margin surgery, she advised me to pay attention to that intuition.

I spoke to Elenna and to OwlSnake and moved closer and closer to a decision. OwlSnake at one point asked intently, "Do you think there is cancer in there?" I said strongly, "no, there is not." And I felt as if I could keep it that way if I tried. I was leaning toward keeping the breast. Then she got the picture that if I did not have the mastectomy, there would be a huge distraction smack dab in the center of my life. I would be worried about it all the time, doing healings on myself, watching, praying, maybe even moving somewhere for treatment. It would keep me from finishing *Strands* or doing any of the other healing work I was supposed to be doing in this lifetime.

I could feel my thinking begin to shift. Now I wondered if a mastectomy was only violent if I resisted it. If I could see it as an offering made so that I could become a better healer and peacemaker, a mastectomy no longer seemed a violent act. My internal warrior of discernment emerged from the mud, pushing for a decision that would, in the end, cause less heartache and would indeed free me to do my work.

I decided to have the mastectomy, to offer a piece of

my flesh as part of this initiation I was entering into. It was a great relief not to be fighting myself anymore. Decision-making had been the hardest part.

While I was clearly trying to approach this differently, I still had much more work to do to get it into my bones, to bring the rest of myself up to speed on this decision. I was not without grief.

I cried when I told my surgeon of my decision. She hates tears and assured me that we could do a reconstruction, and it wouldn't be so bad. She scheduled an appointment with the plastic surgeon. When I was still crying, she suggested we could go ahead and try the margin surgery— maybe it would work. She just couldn't understand that I could decide to go forward this way and still be very upset. And at this point I could not explain it to her. I could barely explain it to myself.

Lucy brought me a four-herb remedy called *Essiac* that she had brewed for me. She had given it to her father when he was diagnosed with prostate cancer, and it had helped him so much. Drinking it every day for three weeks, gave me a core physical strength that is hard to quantify. It seemed to shore me up.

Surgery was scheduled for September 4, the Friday before Labor Day.

COUNCIL OF WOMEN

I was scheduled to go a family reunion at my sister's cabin in eastern Oregon on July 14 and to spend a week, after the reunion, alone with my mother in the cabin.

Over the many years it took me to write *Strands*, I

always advised my mother to avoid reading it. But it had become clear to me that one of the obstacles to the novel's publication was that she had not read it. Sometime before this I had blurted out on the phone that I would like for her to read the book while we were at the cabin alone together. So not only was she going to read it, but I was going to be there as she read it. The idea of her reading it haunted me. I had no idea how she would react to what I had put her character through.

When I told Elenna I had decided to have the mastectomy, she asked if I wanted a circle of women to meet before my trip to Oregon. Neither of us was sure what this would entail, but I said that it sounded like a wonderful idea. The only time we could schedule was the night before I left.

↞

July 11
Dear Sisters,
I have come to the next step in my journey both with the tumor in my breast and with the work of healing the Motherline. Please join me in a women's sacred circle at Elenna's house Tuesday evening from 7-9. Your presence and support there would be greatly appreciated.

This sacred circle joins a larger field that is coalescing, that is calling. In the field are the relationships among the tumor, my breast, the Daré community, healing and peacemaking, women in my life, and my grandmother ancestor Harriet's awakening me to the desire to (as Elenna has stated it so clearly) pull the motherline through into the present.

After much praying, wailing, begging, losing sleep, confusion, information gathering, sacred story/illness work with Elenna, consultation with ancestors through Owl Snake, and consultation with other dear friends, I have decided to have a mastectomy on my right breast. Without this procedure, I feel I would be constantly looking over my shoulder for the time when a cancer could develop and without warn-

ing metastasize and move to any organ of my body through the blood stream. As Owl Snake said to me, "you must pick your battles." While my own health is important to me, it is not what I want as the focus of the rest of my life. I cherish this life and work that I have been given and am willing to offer myself to it.

Part of the work I have been given is the healing of the Motherline, both my own personal strands and the multitude of strands that have been relegated to silence in this culture. The novel I am about to publish is about this subject and gathers as its material the life histories of women in my family—me, my mother, my grandmother and my great-grandmother. On the day after our sacred gathering I leave for a family reunion which will be followed by a week alone with my mother on sacred land in Oregon. My mother will be reading for the first time this novel in which the lead character is based on her. I expect that we will be doing very deep work around the mother-daughter line and that there will be much opportunity for healing.

The hope for this sacred ceremony created on Tuesday is that we will pull through and together all of our motherlines and those of future beings. I cannot say what this ceremony will look like because I do not know.

Please prepare for this circle as you might any sacred gathering, doing whatever work of your own that needs to be done ahead of time so that nothing prevents you from being fully present.

I look forward to seeing all of you and your ancestors there.
In sisterhood and love,
Elise

᭼

July 11 (Deena Metzger's response)
Dear dear Elise:

I have directions. I don't know if I can be with you on my journey up to the Bay Area at the beginning of a one hundred day soul vigil—these words just came to me to use them here even as I try to understand them—

When I decided to have a mastectomy, I wrote similar words -- "While my own health is important to me, it is not what I want as the focus of the rest of my life." I didn't know I would become a healer. Had I tried to keep healing myself on a cellular level, I never would have had the energy or focus for the larger work. I have never regretted that decision. I have always consistently, publicly and in the privacy of my own heart, honored it. The mastectomy was an issue sometimes for a short time. Thirty-two years later, I always forget that my body isn't the norm. So does Michael. What is most important is that I don't live in fear—I live in full, substantiated, unshakable optimism about health and all our futures, including the four leggeds, winged, swimming, standing people.

I hope to be able to be with you. If not, you will know that I will be with you for the entire journey up. My prayers and my hope. But also awe and encouragement - your time with your mother will be blessed; I am certain. This is a new beginning for you — with didg in hand, a walkabout of new beauty.

Love and blessings,
Deena [Metzger]

᚛

Yes! I will definitely be there to support you in this. And working with all the motherlines seems very important to me as well. I look forward to supporting you and of course gathering and weaving what needs to be created. Until then all my blessings and love. I am here if you need to talk at all or be supported.

Love, Lacey

᚛

I am deeply moved by your invitation, and will do my best to prepare with prayers and meditation. As for your next step, my prayers are with you.

What you suggest for the circle is very, very important work for all of us as women. Thank you for the opportunity to support you and open to our own herstories.

Love, Pamela

❧

Without a doubt I will be there. You can call on me for all your needs.
    Love,
    Dipti

❧

I am honored to be asked and will bring whatever is called, even as water whispers in my ear as I write this.
    In Healing, Katie

❧

Dear lovely men of Daré,

    I wanted to let you know that Elenna and I have called for a women's sacred circle on Tuesday evening before I go to Oregon on Wednesday. This sacred circle joins a larger field that is coalescing, that is calling. In the field are the relationships among the tumor, my breast, the Daré community, healing and peacemaking, women in my life, and my grandmother ancestor Harriet's awakening me to the desire to (as Elenna has stated it so clearly) pull the motherline through into the present.

    Though this particular circle is limited to women, I am inviting you, wherever you are that evening, to hold space for us and send us your healing energy, protection and prayers. As always your energies are precious to me and to Daré.

    Love and blessings to you,
    Elise

❧

Dear Elise,
    I will be away from the house on Tuesday evening so the women can be all they can be in surrounding you in healing. Before I leave I will light a large candle from all the Daré men who love you and hold you in prayer.
    Love,
    Garner

❧

My hopes and prayers are with you, Elise. It's a very difficult and brave decision you are taking. Great admiration for your courage. Yes, best not to have to always be looking over your shoulder, wondering.

Bruce

.❧

I was heartened by the responses to the invitation for the women's council. And I was just starting to get my head around the idea of mastectomy when on July 14, I had my appointment with the plastic surgeon. I had been reading about reconstruction and felt as if I would like to have a saline implant. I didn't trust silicone after all the health repercussions from them the last time they were on the market.

I was fairly comfortable with that decision, when the plastic surgeon said that in my case he wouldn't recommend the saline implant (the reasons are spelled later in this narrative) and that I would need to have both breasts done to make them match.

He assured me that they have been having great success with the silicone implants, and that if you take into account the trial period, they have been out on the market for five years with no problems. Five years, I told him, only gets me to fifty-eight.

I called Elenna in a panic because I was about to go away for two weeks, and I just couldn't bear to have another of these decisions unresolved. She called two friends, Karen and Dipti. One had a a double unreconstructed mastectomy. The other had an unreconstructed mastectomy for five years ago; she had recently decided to have reconstruction. Luckily, they were both coming to the women's council that evening and could come early to discuss this with me.

Dipti and Karen spoke to me frankly, saying that no choice I made would be without severe drawbacks—that was the nature of this next move.

I looked at my left breast (well, actually, both of them) with love. They had done nothing wrong. And I couldn't imagine cutting the left one for the sake of some abstract concept called symmetry.

By the time the women's council started, I had come around to believing that I would just have to choose no reconstruction. But it was making me very sad. I felt I would be marked for life and could never go back.

I put this thinking on hold to attend the sacred gathering of women. There were about fifteen women there, and they all brought pictures of their ancestors for the altar. It was beautiful to see all of those faces, mostly women. Elenna had put stones all around the room so that we were held in a circle of stones.

We hadn't had time to plan the gathering, and I had said I didn't want it to be all about me. But I did start things with my story and the story of the novel. In the novel, Emma is adopted at age six and decides she is going to be good from then on in order not be abandoned again. The adoption serves as a metaphor for girls who, through circumstance and socialization, lose themselves as they grow up. We talked about ourselves when we were six and what we gave up to become the people we are. And we spoke of what our ancestors suffered in their lives and how they managed to survive.

I spoke of the novel as a vehicle for healing, just as I hope I could be a vehicle for healing around the mastectomy. What does a vehicle of healing look like? Is it necessarily deformed and asymmetrical? I didn't feel as if I really needed that lesson as I already have deformed feet and as such have never had a "normal" body. So why me? What was it I still needed to learn?

Pamela asked that I read a section of the novel and I opened it like the book was a divination tool. The page I opened to was one where my grandmother's character is talking to her niece. She recites her an Emily Dickenson poem. It is about a tiny bird who falls from the nest. The niece doesn't get the implications of this and laughs. My grandmother's character realizes that the niece has not fallen yet and wants to protect her from it. I related to the niece and felt that my grandmother was speaking those words to me in an effort to protect and comfort me.

It was intensely gratifying to have all these seen women and all of our unseen ancestors come together to send me off for the reading of the novel by my mother and to begin preparations for the next part of my journey with the mastectomy.

Later I wrote these words in my journal: open heart, vulnerable, unrehearsed, all shields are down.

CHAPTER THREE
The Weighing In

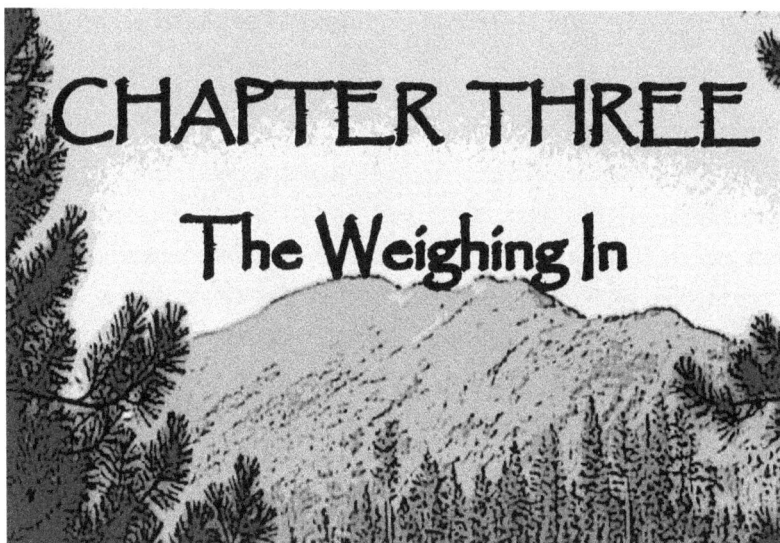

The night of the women's council, I did not sleep. I was grieving my breast and trying to bear the thought of emptiness where a breast should be. How could I possibly become a person like Deena Metzger who could be so public about her disfigurement? I asked myself why being "normal" is so important to me. Who must I become so that it is not? I was desperately trying to hold onto an image of myself as healthy, strong, and normal. Were those things part of who I was? I certainly thought so at the time.

Early the next day, my husband and I flew out of Oakland to Boise, Idaho, where we waited until my mother's plane arrived and then drove three hours to my sister's place in Union, Oregon. Since it was 100 degrees in Boise, we found a park to hang out in. The oppressive heat was no help to my mental state, or my physical one for that matter. I managed to drive us safely to Union and then took a tranquilizer to get some sleep.

Many things happened in Oregon, some of which are described in the letter below. The first part of the trip was a family reunion where at first no one was talking about my situation. Finally, on the last day of the reunion, we talked about it. The discussion started because the women of the family were all sitting around in the cabin. My sister-in-law's mother had died that spring; she looked so raw and vulnerable. I said to her, "You look broken-hearted." She came over to lie beside me on the bed and to cuddle. We talked of her Mom dying and how she is sometimes overwhelmed with sadness. I told her that she looked wise, as if her mother's wisdom had come into her.

Because the energy in the room had softened, the subject of the mastectomy came up naturally. I cried as I told of my limited choices and that I was worrying mainly about the gym, hiding, and the feelings of shame that I associated with hiding. My sister said they would all love me no matter what. It was such a relief to me to have the "elephant in the room" spoken about.

I had brought my grandmother's picture with me to Oregon and made an altar of it during the reunion for all to see, especially my two nieces who did not know the story. One night we had dinner out and someone gave me a sprig of rosemary which I brought back and placed near my grandmother's picture—for remembrance.

After everyone but my mother, Sue's puppy, PJ, and I left, I was teetering on the edge of despair. Yet I was going about my business while my mother read *Strands*. I had many sleepless nights, went through much crying and puzzling over why this was happening. I read Deena Metzger's book *Tree* and it hit close to home. I kept hearing her phrase, "flat as a boy" which she must have said twenty times in the book, or at least it felt that way to me. Now I don't even know why that bothered me so much. *Tree* made me go into that space of fear, grief, disbelief, anger, and horror. Every little feeling seemed amplified, as if I was in a tunnel where feelings reverberated endlessly.

MUSINGS

I wrote all kinds of things, trying to make sense of this experience. I tried poetry:

Beauty in the I
Behold the many layers
of surrender.

❧

Eye behind the I
Sees beyond face value
connecting strands

❧

Face value
head on.
What is important?

Face value, face it now
What is important to you?
What will you regret on your deathbed?
Pay attention to that now while you still
Embody an instrument.
Take a deep belly breath
let yourself be played.

❧

Time and Chance Happeneth to Us All

When I lose a breast
what will counterbalance?
What needs to grow bigger, more spacious
to bear the disfigurement
to balance the asymmetry?

A stronger heart,
A spirit short on vanity
who loses false faith in the itty bitty Elise?

Petite Elise.

A spirit who does not lean forward
into a future wicked with trouble.
One who travels far past face value.

Face value
Look it right in the eyes
Yes, I scream, I know what I value.
Sun glinting off pine needles
Grasses blowing gently in the wind.
Sunset over the mountain
Dog's unrestrained joy
Deep and full breath.
Sounds of music guided by listening
360 degrees of bird song.
Story that teaches me something about what to value.
Presence of friends

Support of family.
Eyes that notice all forms of beauty
Smell of mint, rosemary and sage.
Love in all its forms.

Perfect balance is stasis—nothing can change.
A state in which there is neither motion
nor development
often results from opposing forces balancing each other.
When opposing forces suddenly do not have balance,
there is a shift from stasis.
To movement.
To change.
Time and chance happeneth to us all.

∾

Conformity,
deformity
Where is thy sting?

∾

cleave [kleev][1]

1. split: to split, or make something split, especially along a plane of natural weakness
2. cut path through something: to make a way through something (literary)
3. penetrate something: to penetrate or pierce something deep or dense such as water or heavy undergrowth (literary)

[Old English < Indo-European]
-cleav•a•ble, adj

---

1   Encarta ® World English Dictionary © & (P) 1998-2005 Microsoft Corporation.

cleav•age
(plural cleav•ages) n

1. crease visible between breasts: the hollow visible between a woman's breasts when a low-cut garment is worn
2. split in something: a split, division, or separation of something
3. act of splitting: division or splitting
4. geology minerals rock or mineral fracture: the splitting of minerals or rocks along natural planes of weakness determined by their internal crystal lattice.
The angle of cleavage is one of the features used to identify minerals.
5. embryology repeated division of fertilized egg: the repeated division of a fertilized ovum zygote before formation of the early embryo blastula.
The zygote does not increase in size during this process because the cells become progressively smaller after each division.
6. chemistry splitting of molecule: the splitting of a molecule into simpler molecules through the breaking of a chemical bond

cleav•er
(plural cleav•ers) n

heavy knife used by butchers: a heavy knife with a broad blade, used by butchers

From robust to no bust

ro•bust

1. strong and healthy: strong, healthy, and hardy in constitution
2. strongly constructed: built, constructed, or designed to be sturdy, durable, or hard-wearing
3. needing physical strength: involving or requiring great physical strength and stamina
Football is a robust sport.
4. determined: characterized by firmness and determination and a re-

fusal to make concessions; a robust defense
 5. straightforward: showing clear thought and common sense
6. blunt or crude: rough and direct or crude
7. full-flavored: rich, strong-tasting, and full-bodied
8. capable of recovery: describes a computer program or system that
is able to recover from unexpected conditions during operation
a robust operating system

[Mid-16th century. < Latin robustus "made of oak, hard, strong" <
robur "oak tree, hardness, strength"]

ॐ

Level the playing field of femininity.
Take away the symbols
the clanging
the difference.
Start over and grow something new.
Too many things built this identity
clutter it with illusion.
Start over.
From scratch
from wound,
from flat as a boy—
we were all there once.

Start over.
Reimagine everything about being a woman.
Grow that garden differently
It's not what you think.
Not the heart of the matter
but the heart of the Spirit that matters.
Let nothing tell us differently.

ॐ

One day near the end of the stay, I woke up with a different feeling. In my journal I wrote, "I am going to see this flat space as a badge of courage, as proof of initiation. I am not going to be ashamed of it. I am going to think of myself as pregnant or its opposite—I will be losing something instead of adding. But the anxiety about how I will feel after can just calm down. Just as a woman having a baby does not know how she will feel once the baby is born and her body is so changed, neither do I know or can I know how I will feel. It is best not to project into the future.

Self-conscious—just look at that word. Self, ego, vanity, shame, embarrassment—all of these come from the itty bitty Elise. Really, how bad is this? This body I am using will only have one breast. So I told myself to think of the monk who had only one tooth and smiled all the time. He was not concerned with how he looked but appreciated what function he did have left. I should not, in the end, lose any vital function.

I had brought a novel with me to read, and it turned out to be about a tattoo artist. I wondered if maybe I would get a tattoo so that there would be something where my breast used to be, not just a blank space, an empty page. Then when I got on the plane to go home, I saw a woman coming down the aisle and knew she would sit next to me. She was covered in tattoos. She did indeed sit next to me and we proceeded to have a long conversation about tattoos. She was very concerned about cleanliness and ethics. I left with her card in tow in case I decided to go that route. I didn't tell her anything about myself but just kept the knowledge to myself like a piece of chocolate.

The Return

I returned to find a surprise birthday party for me that my husband Adam had arranged. He had told people he wanted something positive since my birthday had basically come and gone with little fuss while I was in Oregon. I did the best I could to have fun at the party, but with no one talking about the impending surgery, I felt strange.

At that point in time, I could not handle it if my predicament was not acknowledged in some way. I didn't have to talk about it constantly, but I felt horrible, as if I might burst, if I had to ignore it. And, of course, some people wanted nothing more than to ignore it.

After I returned home, I wrote the following letter to friends. It gives more details of what happened during the next week and a half I was in Oregon.

～

August 5
Dear beloved folk,

Before my trip to Oregon on July 15, a group of women met in sacred council to create a space to heal our ancestral lines but particularly our Motherlines. Men blessed the space with a candle and a prayer sculpture and held a protective energy that night. Not all of you could be there in body but were with us in Spirit.

I wanted to give you an update on what happened in Oregon and on my surgery which is now scheduled for September 4 (what time of day I won't know until the day before surgery).

My family reunion was emotional but good. I was able to talk to my family about the upcoming mastectomy and I received a lot of support. My own emotional space was very up and down as it continues to be. I never know when I am going to begin crying or feel totally exhausted.

After most of the family left and it was just my mother and me in the cabin for a week, she read my novel Strands and I read Deena Metger's Tree, her writing about her own journey through breast cancer and a mastectomy.

First, my mother's reading of Strands was an incredibly humbling and heartening experience. Before I handed it to her, we talked briefly about what I felt the book was about: that I am using the facts of our lives as a vehicle for healing both our own Motherline (four generations of women in my family) and the healing of our society's so-often ruptured Motherlines. She cried even before she began reading saying that every time she thinks of her mother's life, she cries. I didn't even know that. In fact, what is remarkable is how little I did know of what I was actually doing in writing Strands.

My mother would sometimes pause and ask if something I wrote was true or if I made it up. At one point she asked if the part where her mother says she always loved her daughter and that she fought to keep her was true. Tears welled up in my eyes and I answered that I was pretty sure that was true. This became the first time she actually got the message that her mother loved her! I had no idea that I had become the deliverer of that crucial message and that it is most likely one of the reasons I wrote the book.

She loved the book! And she keeps thanking me for letting her read it. (I had always said when I was writing it that she should just not read it, mainly because I didn't know how she would take it). I asked her lately after she thanked me again, just what it was that she liked about it. She answered in her simple way, "It was organized so well." I translate that to mean that her story now has a coherence it never had before. All of us have memories of the past and our memories play tricks with us so maybe this story is as true as other people's stories of their pasts are—fact mixed with fiction mixed with analysis. She will be processing the stories for a while to come and so will I.

Now as for me reading Tree, it was, as you might imagine,

not easy for me, especially the part describing Deena's feelings post-operation—every time I project into my own future, I am wracked with tears and wondering if I can stand to be marked for life, wondering if I will be able to tolerate what I see in the mirror every day.

The day of the gathering of Council of Sisters and Ancestors, I met with the plastic surgeon and was told that because of my neuro-muscular disease (which came from my fatherline), I am not a candidate for a saline implant which would require embedding in the muscle, thereby compromising the muscle and making it less strong for such things as crutch use which realistically is likely a part of my future. I am very clear that I am not in a position to bargain away any good muscles since so many of the ones I have are already compromised. The only real option then, besides not reconstructing, is a silicone implant, unembedded, and surgery on the left breast to make it match the right side, thereby in essence destroying the sensitivity in that breast as well and scarring it in three places.

As I look at my left breast, I feel I do not have it in me to destroy the life in it in order to look okay in clothes. Because I still won't look good naked, that's for sure, with scaring on both sides. And a silicone implant represents to me a risk of leakage that I cannot tolerate right now. So I am choosing not to have reconstruction.

Mostly I worry about how I will deal with the Y where I go nearly every day to swim. Before this happened to me, I often wondered: where are the women who had mastectomies? I know they exist in Berkeley and the Bay Area in even more numbers than other places but I never see evidence of them at the Y. So either women who have them stop coming or they are hiding.

I need to swim at the Y. I cannot rely on other forms of exercise—they just don't work for me. And I am pretty sure that I cannot stand to hide. I can try to convince myself that I just want my privacy, but in my heart I know that for me hiding triggers a state of shame in which I am not willing to live.

I said to Elenna the other day that one of my friends cannot seem to talk to me about any of this and just acts as if nothing out of the ordinary is happening. I know we have danced this dance before with issues that were difficult; we would both paint flowers around the edges of the room, only pausing when the shadow of the elephant got into our light and then quickly moving to a different place where the light was more cheery. Only now I am the elephant. I've got nowhere to flee to.

And the elephant is what I think I will be at the Y. Whether women can deal with that (and whether I can) is yet to be seen but all of us will be confronted with it. And maybe we can finally glimpse the wall to wall elephants that are already in that room. So many of us are ashamed of some aspect of our bodies. Maybe we can come out of the edges and even climb up on those elephants. What a powerful bunch we would be then!

I know that this circumstance that I find myself in is medicine, that this is the initiation of a healer. And I am trying to become that healer. I am scheduled to start a Sound, Voice, and Music Healing certificate program two weeks after surgery. These two things are intimately connected and I can see part of that even from where I stand, pre-surgery. I see how resistant I am to being perceived as sick. I am living in a strange borderland between sickness and health. I do not have cancer but I have the seeds of cancer in me and must do what is necessary to keep the cancer from developing. What an intriguing place of uncertainty and drastic action! Technically, they call this a breast cancer, but at the same time, I do not have cancer.

This place I stand is a place of hope. It is where we stand as a culture. We do not have to die as a culture, if we take drastic action now. But if we do not take that action, we risk a sudden incident of metasticization that will indeed attack one of our vital functions and kill us.

We have to make value decisions immediately. What is important to us? Is it so important to conform, fit in, be a good consumer, buying products that make us look young and beautiful, waging war so that our way of life can continue unabated? Or are we actually yearning to be seen through, to be recognized as who we are beneath and in our flaws and differences and connections?

To be marked forever as imperfect is to forfeit that dubious goal of perfection in body and to see through it to the acceptance of the natural cycles of aging and death and rebirth and receive the concurrent offerings of healing, love and creativity. What is offered is a way to stand in a state of curiosity about what lies beneath and to live in that place where we are all connected to each other and to the rest of the natural world. When can we finally resume our natural place, not as destroyers but as the vehicles for life, for beauty, connection and healing to become conscious of itself?

I am battered by the ions of negative and positive, of black and white, of right and wrong, of life and death. With all that I am and all that I have, I ask to learn how to live in the rainbow of uncertainty, in the constantly shifting borderlands, not of knowledge, but of eternal recognition of and gratitude for the gift of life that has been given to me. And I need all my relations for that. I need all of you for that. Your prayers are indeed welcome as I make my way through this between now and Sept. 4 and beyond.

May we all be healthy,
Elise

꤮

August 5

Excellent! Thank you so much for sharing your message that you have come this lifetime to share. It is one of courage. I love and cherish you for saying "yes" to this mighty work, and I am here to support you all along the way.
much love and light,
OwlSnake (robbie)

꤮

Dear Elise,
Thank you for putting such beautiful words

to your Motherline Story and your own Story. I am deeply and profoundly touched. I can relate to so much with such sincere feelings.

I sit with tears and courage for you and us women. Thank you for sharing with us.

Love and Blessings,
Dipti

∾

August 9

Dearest Friends of Elise:

I have been dreaming of Elise for the past three nights. The night of the full moon I woke at 3 am and wrote this poem. I am not a great dreamer, and the fact that the dreams were so filled with Celtic spirit animals was startling. I've done a lot of research into the significance of animals in Celtic lore and these are most interesting to me.

The predominant animals are frogs (healing) and crows (the Otherworld connection). I realize the importance of the circumstance and the depth of this quest Elise is on and am honoring this in the poem. In my first book, there is a poem called "Für Elise," so this is "Für Elise II." I wanted to share this poem with all who care for and are cared for by our friend and sister, Elise. This is a difficult journey for Elise, and for all who love her, so I honor her in this poem and my heart.

All Love and Grace,
Meg Withers
(poem printed at beginning of Introduction)

∾

Dear Elise,

Thank you for being willing to share this with me even though you do not know me that well. It is beautifully written and I hope someday your novel will be available for others to also read. I, for one, hope to have that opportunity at some point. Your time with your mother and the way you have worked is also beautiful to see from what you wrote.

You are poised at an amazing place and are articulating that so well. I hope that you will be able to walk into the Y and swim with the elegance that comes from knowing your decisions and life have beauty and integrity and truth....

love
Brenda

❧

Dear Elise,

I read the phrase, far down in the letter "I don't have cancer" with great relief. But feel sad that the prevention is so drastic.

It is something how proud we are of looks. Once I went to a costume party, and was self conscious that my costume was different than everyone else's. Then I danced with the blind salsa teacher. She gave me a lesson!

Gael

❧

Peeps,

My God, what an emotional roller coaster you are on.

It seems that so much of the difficulty with our lives is our inability to truly accept what we can't change. We keep groping, longing for everything to turn out the way we have envisioned it. Of course, sometimes it does but there are the times when it does not. To accept what is and to live in the present, the Now, is such a wonderful ideal but sooo difficult to actually DO!

All my love to you, Adam and your Mother.
Connie

❧

it's all in the continuum; the work is already happening, and each of our initiations is an important part, whether or not we speak of them. yes, the goddess is stretching her wings and her soul across the ethers as the veil is being torn away... Yolanda

❧

Meg, thank you so much for your beautiful poem. It is significant that you dreamt for 3 nights of Elise, and woke at 3 in the morning to write this poem. Three is a powerful number in Celtic worldview—it symbolizes the three forms of female power: the virgin, the mother, and the crone. It is also the number of nights the moon is dark as it changes from waning to waxing, and the moon is associated with Artemis, the silver-bow wielding protector of animals from the male hunters.

It is wonderful to be reminded that it was the right breast that was removed in preparation for becoming an Amazon warrior, to protect the safety of women. I feel that the opening we made for all of our mother lines reaches back all the way to these ancient times, when women were in right relationship to their own power.

May the ripples of this work, the blessings that Elise's courage to share brought forth, continue to sustain us for a long, long time. Even for those of you who weren't part of that circle in body, as part of the wider circle surrounding Elise, I believe your Motherline is becoming activated.

Maybe Elise and her ancestors have provided the very seed we needed to begin our work together as women—what are the possibilities?

Much love,
Cynthia

❧

Dear Elise,

Your account of your process moved me to tears. As for your resolution— "...to forfeit that dubious goal of perfection in body and to see through it to the acceptance of the natural cycles of aging and death and rebirth and receive the concurrent offerings of healing, love and creativity..." May it be so.

Please call on me for anything you need.

Love,

Jane

❧

Dear Elise,

I will be your elephant at the Y next Thursday. Together we will see what it is like when a woman who has mastectomy scars does not hide, when a woman who has not had reconstruction after mastectomy does not hide. Together we will discover courage and shed even the lightest notion of shame.

I write this publicly because I am not wholly courageous nor without shame and know that by speaking this truth into the community, strength will find its way.

With love,

~Karen

❧

Dear Elise,

Thank you so much for sending me your lovely letter! All I can say is Wow!! Your reflections cannot but affect us all as you embrace this new journey in your life. I am amazed at the deepness of your heart-mind, world vision. As always all your beauty shines bright and is eternal.

Thank you for bringing stars to my eyes.

Love, Pemba

❧

Dear Elise, sisters and ancestors,

Thank you THANK you THANK YOU! For your

heartfelt and conscious journey into healing that is so eloquently not just your own... generous, profound and vital are words that come to mind.

As for the Y, well—you know I have a particularly strong sense there, and there are Mandlovu's[2] in that locker room, oh yes indeedy, who are not afraid and do not hide! Berkeley Y is an outrageously powerful place for being all who you are...and I feel your genuine concern of showing up as who you are becoming is present as well.

Remembering my days at the Berkeley Y, where notices of all kinds make their way to the boards...you can post a notice asking for other women members who have traveled the road that you are embarking on, to have a meeting of the hearts in the locker room—you will be amazed before you are halfway through! There is a Y member, Kelly Corrigan, a writer and photographer, who just published a widely appraised book The Middle Place, about her journey through Breast Cancer as her father was going through cancer (hmmm meeting of the father and mother lines yet again!).

Just some threads here to weave into your tapestry! -I am so honored to be on this journey with you and please, call me anytime to talk to muse to cry to laugh—I welcome it!

Love,
Katie

❧

Dear Elise
You write beautifully and articulately about the range and depth of your experience. I am happy to read about your going ahead with

---

2   MaNdlovu is the word the Ndebele people of Zimbabwe use for a female elephant.

the certificate program in sound healing.
   Blessed be,
   Lucy C

❧

   This is so beautiful, Elise. Thank you for sharing it. We are all so vulnerable, and so is our way of life and the planet. You are a way-shower. Health to you!
   Love,
   Juli

❧

   thanks for including me in your poignant e-mail... I offer a [bodywork] session to you when you need it, A gift from an old friend.
   sincerely,
   Viviane

❧

Elise,
   Thank you for letting me know what's been happening and how things are going for you. I am touched by your courage, your ability to be real, grounded with and express of all the feelings. So much! You really are a peaceful warrior. I will be holding you in my heart and expecting more miracles.
   Love
   Brigid

❧

Dear Elise-
   I am at Spirit Rock on the family retreat, and just doing a brief once over of my e-mails. I thank you so very much for contacting me personally with your news. I want you to know first off that I 100% support your choice around the surgery, and your reasons for it—for what that's worth. Devastating tho it must be, it seems that it will deal with a lot of uncertainty and prolonged decision making, and, as you say, you don't want to make this the focus of your life.

You have much else to do and be here!

   Impermanence ...of our bodies, our health, "life as we know it." Today Ajahn Amaro was reminding us of the Buddha's 5 reminders, which (rough paraphrase) are:

I am of the nature to grow old
I am of the nature to have illness
I am of the nature to die
I am of the nature of losing all things that I hold dear, sooner or later
(Can't remember the 5th—maybe it's I am of the nature to forget long lists of wise sayings!)

   So, somewhere beyond the why me and goddammit and not now and this sucks is, I know, in you, in me, the wisdom and awareness that we are all of a nature to pass out of stages of health, happiness, balance, into stages of loss, instability and pain (and then on to whatever is next). I'm sorry this is happening to you. I feel your strength coming through your letter.

   You have so many resources. I hope I see you soon, and let me know in advance what kind of help and support would be good for you before and after surgery, OK?

   With love and tenderness,
   Betsy

❦

The responses to my letter were heartening. I was surprised that e-mail could be so powerful a tool in community and support, that what might have seemed a cold technology could provide such warmth. I couldn't possibly have sent that many individual letters or had that many conversations, but I could easily send and then read e-mail responses. Though I got feedback from one friend that she couldn't stand to read such intense missives on e-mail, most people not only seemed to be able to do it, they did it well.

I had a dream around that time: *I am driving and a hummingbird flies into the window of the car. It is large and not showy (reminded me of something I had seen at Sue's property in Oregon). I open the passenger window to make sure it has an escape route if it wants it, but it sits on my right shoulder and snuggles up against my neck.*

I wonder if it is a message from my grandmother, as I feel that she sits on my injured shoulder waiting for me to finish the novel.

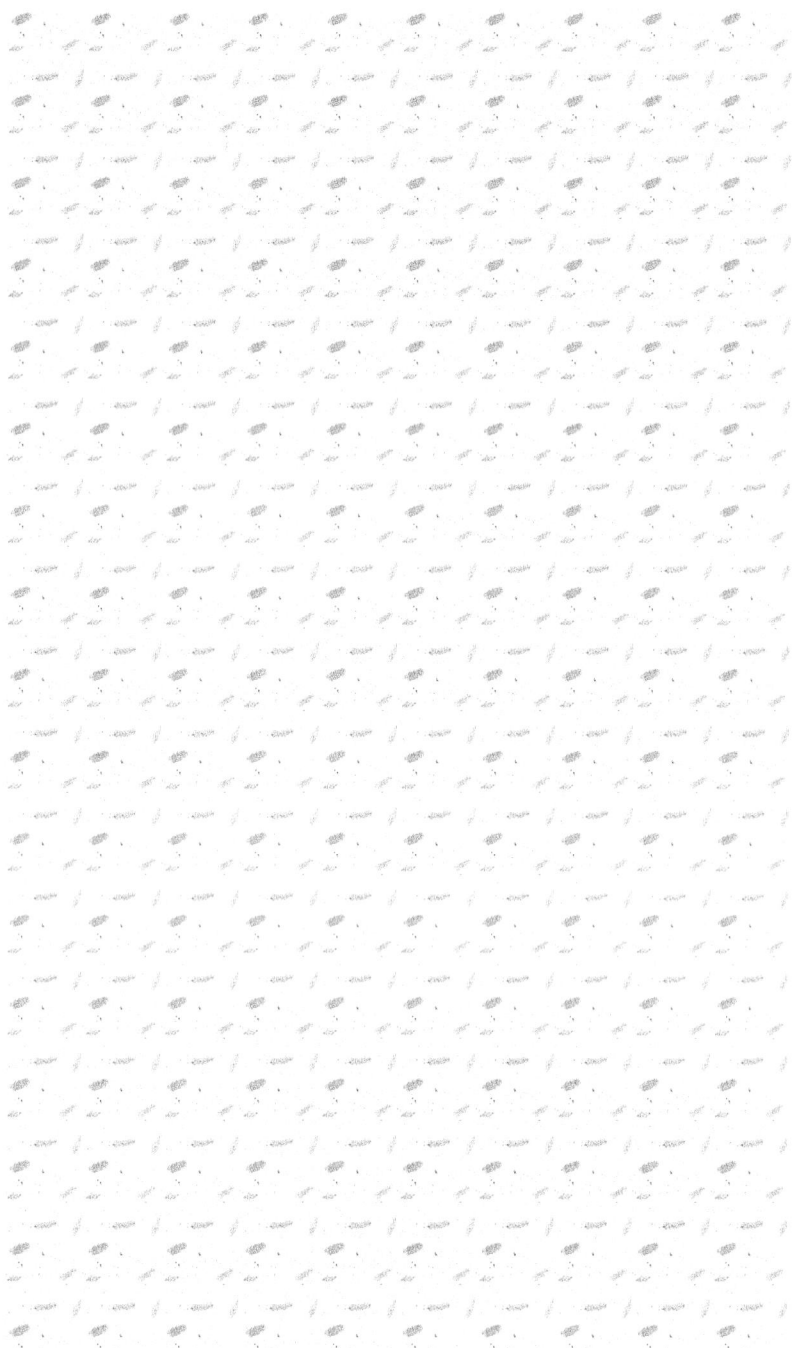

CHAPTER FOUR

Preparations

Photo Credit: Kurt Anderson

I had about one month from the date of that letter to the surgery, and I felt the need to use the time to prepare myself for what was to come. I did not know how one went about such preparations but I started anyway. Elenna left for Washington for a training on the four directions. Having relied on her heavily, I was now left to my own devices for a while. I was feeling more resolved since all of the decisions regarding the surgery had been made. But I wondered how to use this special time period before surgery.

At that point I was not making any commitments for after surgery. I felt as if I would be a different person and I didn't want to make commitments for that person I would become. The only thing I knew I would be doing was the sound healing class—that I knew I would do.

Throughout all of my preparations, I continued my morning practice of yoga, meditation, and playing the didgeridoo to call in the directions. This daily practice helped to ground me each day.

The Daré community was getting very busy with the preparations to host Mandaza Kandemwe, the Zimbabwean shaman in whose lineage the Daré was founded. He visits yearly, and we are responsible for setting up events in which he will participate. This year there was more than usual happening with the community (not just my crisis but several other crises among key members of the group.) I continued volunteering for tasks, even though I did not know how much I could do. I was breaking down at the oddest moments and didn't know if I could be relied upon for anything.

LESSONS LEARNED

I remember stopping in at a cosmetics shop to pick up something for a friend. I was overwhelmed by the number of products they carry. There was a woman at the counter trying several different colors of makeup; she became frustrated because none of them seemed to match exactly. She had about three clerks running around trying to help her.

I remember looking at her and screaming inside, thinking that she was the one who needed this lesson in vanity, not me. I told myself I had already gotten over the vanity thing if I ever had it. At that moment, I thought the lesson one would learn by having one's breast cut off might be to stop worrying about how one looks. If so, damn it, she needed it more than I did! I carried that rage around for a while, until it seemed to fade away. That's what I mean, though, about not being in control of my feelings. It was not pretty.

I started waking up in the middle of the night and having visions of the surgery. I would lie awake for what seemed like hours and watch as I looked down on the operating table from above and watched the flesh being cut off. It was not nightmarish for some reason but seemed to be like training films to get me ready. It reminds me of the Buddhists who meditate by staring at dead bodies and seeing them in various stage of decomposure to remind them of the impermanence of life. It went on for about a week and then stopped.

I was experiencing lessons coming at me from all directions. One evening I went to a meditation at Spirit Rock led by Eve Decker, a singer/song-writer and Buddhist teacher. She mentioned that once when she was in great turmoil in her life, she was at a retreat doing walking meditation. The place she chose to walk had a blank wall at one end which some would consider boring or ugly. But she saw it as a place of peace, a place without drama. I thought, that is what my chest *sans* breast could be, too, a place of peace, no drama, a blank wall.

A guy in the hot tub was talking one day and told his story of how he fell off a ledge while at work and he now has a metal rod up his spine. He said he looked okay on the outside, but on the inside he was completely changed. He now prays in gratitude every day.

I went to *Julie & Julia*, the Julia Child movie, and found in her a person who was totally without self-consciousness; I loved her for it and saw her as a role model. She was abnormally tall and rather awkward and she made no apologies for it whatsoever and, in fact, became very successful.

Karen (who had a double mastectomy five years before) accompanied me to swim at the Y. Though I know it
was hard for her, she did not flinch and broke the ice in the
locker room, although for the most part, no one seemed
to notice. She showered outside a stall, in a line of showers.
We emerged triumphant. Freedom! The charge seemed to
be gone, maybe?

I usually attend a five-day Buddhist silent retreat for
women at Mount Tamalpais the last weekend of August. This
year the dates exactly corresponded to Mandaza's visit and
for the longest time I couldn't decide what to do. Finally,
because the Daré community had been so helpful to me
through all of this, I knew I had to be there for Mandaza's
visit. I made the decision before the surgery was scheduled
and when I looked at the timing of his visit, I was amazed.
I would be in ritual work with Mandaza right up until my
surgery. In fact, his last day in Oakland would be the day of
my surgery. What timing! So I did what I could to help set
up the events.

The largest event was to take place the Sunday before my surgery. I attended meetings during this time and
worked to get out flyers and generally spread the word
about his visit.

When Elenna returned from her trip to Washington, we went for a walk at the Marina in Berkeley, a place
we often find great inspiration. She filled me in on some of
what she had learned about the four directions.

At some point she asked me if I planned to do a ritual before my surgery. I bristled at the thought: one more
thing I needed to do, and I had no idea how I would do that.
She mentioned that I might want to do something with the

direction of East, new beginnings. I pictured myself going out into nature at dawn the day before my surgery and praying. That seemed all right. Then she said that she would like to be there to welcome me back. I couldn't imagine asking her to be somewhere at dawn. I let it just sit with me a while to see what might arise.

My friend Lucy and I had a little time that day to meet down on the waterfront in the City. We did a divination with the Mother of Peace Tarot deck. We spent some time deciphering the cards and just catching up and being in each others' presence.

On the way home, I wrote in my journal: "I feel I have lived a whole lifetime in one morning. Such love, such care from them both. I am so fortunate. I am learning so much."

On August 15, OwlSnake led a workshop on the ancestors. We set up altars for our ancestors and, of course, I focused on Harriet, my grandmother. The doctors had told me that my tumor was most likely related to the fall I had had when I injured my arm. They felt that the fall probably jarred the breast and perhaps stimulated the body to make a protective coating around the tumor, thus making it detectable.

At some point OwlSnake had told me she thought Harriet had been the instigator behind the fall so that the tumor would be found and taken care of and would not interfere with my work, first the novel and then more, maybe the sound healing work and other writing.

So I set up the altar for Harriet (OwlSnake had started calling her Harry, and come to think of it, that is probably what she went by in some circles.) There were a number of Daré members there and at the end I was feeling very sad. I don't know if it was because I was thinking of Harriet or my own condition, but I began to cry. Daré members gathered around me, and one of them suggested that we needed to take the grief to the water which was only a few blocks away.

Four of us, dressed all in white for the workshop, traipsed down to Alameda Beach. When we walked out onto the beach, it must have looked like we were there for a ritual of some sort. Maybe we were.

We said to each other that it was too bad we didn't have our swimming suits; the water looked so inviting. Then the next thing we knew, three of us were in the water fully dressed in our white outfits, a baptism of sorts. The fourth person stayed with the extra clothes we were able to throw off. We three became like small children, laughing, screaming, singing, rocking each other in the small waves. We lost all sense of self-consciousness and simply relished the present with each other. To look into the other two faces and see such glee, such relaxed and clear joy was to look in the mirror and see my face, too. This was what it felt like to shed my vanity, my self-consciousness. Such a lesson learned so easily and with so much joy!

Since we didn't have towels and the wind was chilly, we lay down directly on the sand where it was warm, making a total mess of our lovely white clothes. We used whatever was available to warm ourselves, not caring what an adult would do. Later, when we were warm, we got ice cream, and later still went to dip ourselves in a hot tub at a health club. It was a spontaneity that I have not known in a long time. And it felt like a rite of passage.

PLANNING RITUALS

I had been talking to various people about the ritual I was planning. Each time I spoke of it, it more became clear to me. To someone I said, "I'm thinking of having it on a mountain at dawn." In conversation with someone else, I said, "Yes, I think I will have it on Inspiration Point Trail at the point at which you can look one way and see Mount Tamalpais and the other way, east, and see Mount Diablo."

A little later, I spoke to someone and said that I felt that I needed men there. I didn't know why I wanted that ritual to be composed mostly of men. I knew I was asking a lot of anyone—to be there at dawn. Since it was the week of Mandaza's visit, most of them would be quite busy but I went ahead and wrote the following letters:

❧

Dear Alan and Garner,

I have a special favor to ask of you and you are free as birds to say no if it is too much. But I am going to do a ceremony at dawn on Thursday, September 3, the day before my surgery, and I would like to go up on the Inspiration Point Trail in Tilden to the point where I can see both Mt. Tamalpais and Mt. Diablo. For some reason, what keeps coming to me is that I want to have protection and music from the men in my community. And I wonder if you might come and drum and didge and whatever else while I do this ceremony that I need to do.

Adam will be coming. But Garner, if you are too exhausted from the week of Mandaza's visit, I will truly understand.

Let me know what you think and if it is possible for you to attend.

Thanks so much for all of your support so far and your continued support.
        Love,
        Elise

࣌

Dear Joseph,
        As you know, I am having a mastectomy on Sept. 4. On Sept. 3, I am planning a ritual at dawn up on the Inspiration Point trail in Tilden Park. For some reason as I thought about this ritual, it came to me that I mainly needed to have men there for protection, courage and music. I asked Garner, Alan, and Adam (all of whom can come).
        I know this is a lot to ask and you have many commitments but I would love it if you could also be there. Please feel free to say no. I think it is your fierce protectiveness that I am drawn to at this time.   Let me know what you think.
        Love,
        Elise

࣌

All the men were quick to agree to participate and even seemed appreciative that I asked them. And my husband Adam who is skeptical yet open-minded about these sorts of things, volunteered to come and be part of it. At that point I still didn't know why I was asking men or what I would do with them. But somehow it just seemed that what was to be done would show itself in good time.

I had a pre-surgery appointment, a ritual forced on me by the medical establishment at Kaiser. I didn't realize that it would take three hours to visit different people in various departments. It was a horrible morning. I went alone. If I had it to do again, I would take someone along even though it would be boring for them. But I needed a person who cared about me specifically, not this series of people who smiled vacantly, showing, as a friend of mine likes to say, only the outside of their eyeballs—no human connection there. It was meant to be efficient but it felt mechanistic, inhuman. No one even seemed to know what operation I was having. All of us patients appeared to be interchangeable. I went to my car and cried all the way home. It was apparent that I needed to create my own rituals if I wanted to find meaning in this experience.

Knowing how over-worked everyone in the Kaiser system seemed, I wrote this e-mail to my doctor:

≈

Dear V,

I will be your patient (mastectomy, no-reconstruction) on Sept. 4. I imagine it is a fairly routine operation for you but, of course, for me, it is life-changing.

I have seen how quickly you move through the world and how pushed you are for time. I am sorry it is like that for you.

I ask that before you make the cut and before you sew it up, that you stop and breathe, slow down and think of beauty and of healing.

I will live with this scar for the rest of my life. I would like to know that it was made with awareness and consciousness. If I were conscious, I would make the removal of this breast an offering for the sake of healing. As the one who will be conscious during this time, I ask that you stand in for me.

Thanks so much for all you do—you chose a difficult specialty and I know you are committed and do your job very well.

> *"Let the beauty you love be what you do; there are thousands of ways to kneel and kiss the earth."*
> *—Rumi*

Peace,
Elise

ֆֈ

The community event with Mandaza went very well. I played didgeridoo in the calling of the directions and at the break. There was a community council in which people talked about the violence in our communities and any wisdom they had to share about it. Mandaza conducted healings with individuals with the community as witness. I did not avail myself of this individually but absorbed the healing field created by the event. By this time I was having to protect my energy. Luckily others stepped forward for set up and cleanup.

I had organized a water ritual that Mandaza would lead on Tuesday, September 1, a beautiful day, sunny and calm. I was teary when the ritual began, sad and scared. We talked together, prayed and meditated. At one point each of us was buried in the sand up to our heads and when we were ready, we went into the water. A baptism. At some point the words "enough tears" came to me, a message to stop thinking of this as a funeral and see it as a celebration. That felt right though I wasn't sure how to do that.

After the ritual, my friend Lucy had planned to make a plaster cast of my upper torso right there on the beach. Because of work she couldn't attend the water ritual but while we were still meeting, she made many trips to and from the car to bring the set-up for this casting. She even had a stove to heat water to put the strips of plaster in to wet it. Several women from the ritual stayed and helped us with this task. In all, five women (with Adam there as witness) worked to get the strips even and to make the cast work.

We weren't sure how to make the plaster go all the

way around me and remove it easily. We thought of just doing the front, but I wanted it to go all the way around so that it could be free-standing. Since I have had many casts made of my feet for braces, I knew that by placing a rubber tube under the plaster, it is then possible to cut it along the rubber and not harm the skin. Funnily enough, there was a piece of seaweed (the tail-end of a bull whip kelp) that looked exactly like the rubber the brace-maker uses. That worked great. I felt acknowledged and supported once again as they wound and rubbed and fussed over wrinkles and considered how to proceed.

Photo Credit:
Nicki Koethner

After the cast was cut off, we took pictures of it perched on a rock dressed up in various ways, and we took pictures of my naked breasts for remembrance. I had to go in the water again to rinse off the cast material and had yet another baptism. The ocean cooperated beautifully and was not even terribly cold. I took that cast home and made an altar out of it. I put fresh flowers in it, a torso with flowers arising out of it. Something akin to the phoenix?

Fifty Fingers

Between water ritual and
one facing mountains
ten hands, fifty fingers
create ritual on this sheltered
corner of beach

Under full sun, wind rising
pushing a gentle tide,
strips mummifying her torso
plaster just right for layering
she between tears as they labor

Five pair, ten hands, fifty fingers

smoothing, kneading, layering
five faces focus intent
to preserve shape that was

The five stand away a moment only
One with scissors slits back
from waist to neck

she breathes easier

fingers join in delicate removal
fear a break, collapse or that
their mix might stick

The test: it comes off cleanly
and stands firm!

I join circle of hands
watch as she lay torso naked against a
giant rock, cast on rock above her head
filled with seaweed, flowers, scarf flows
eyes closed; face bright, glows

"I offer up this breast for life."

There would be more tears.

While ours mourn
a loss, would hers seek
and find gain?
                    —Adam David Miller[1]
                         ॐ

When Elenna was in Washington, she had been bit by something, most likely a spider, on her right breast and it had become very swollen. About the same time, Alexis, another Daré member had had a dream in which a spider had bitten her right breast.

These instances of the marking of the right breast in our community made me think that the breast, though it was definitely mine, was also a breast that was being offered from our community. I began to conceive of the notion that I would offer my breast for the nurturance of all beings (a Buddhist expression) or for All of Our Relations (a Native American expression with the possible connection to grandmother spider, weaver of all of our relations).

---
[1]   See www.AdamDavidMillerPoet.com.

In both instances, the offering was for something outside of myself, for the benefit of others.

The next day I went into silence except for words spoken in ritual space. Adam and I had a private appointment with Mandaza that evening. Mandaza basically said that I was doing everything I could, and it sure felt that way. I could feel Mandaza's prayers for me.

The next day was the dawn ritual and I wrote this letter to the participants:

❧

September 2
Dear lovely souls,

I can't tell you how much it means to me that you will be there tomorrow. I am still meditating and praying about how to proceed tomorrow. This much seems to be clear: We meet at 6:00 am in the parking lot of the Inspiration Point Trail.

The prayer I have at the moment is that this breast I am offering for healing is given for the nurturance of All of Our Relations. Please bring an item for the altar that is significant to you in relation to this ceremony.

Last night it came to me: the spider that both Alexis and Elenna have encountered that has bitten their right breasts is a message from Grandmother Spider that the breast that is coming out of our community is to be given in service of the grandmothers and to the web of All of Our Relations.

I will be at the spot a little further down the path where the two sacred mountains can be seen from one place. The men who are there at the beginning of the ritual will give me away as a father does a bride, and I will in turn be giving away the breast. I will pray, make offerings and play the didge. When I am done, I will return to the meadow and ask that you greet me with celebration and music.

This is a time for rejoicing.

After we are done there, Adam and I would like to take every-one out to breakfast in Berkeley.

I am in silence except for the visit with Mandaza this evening so unless you have an emergency question, please e-mail me. I will pick up the phone if I am here and there is something urgent.

Much love to you all,

Elise

❧

Now did I think that I would be able to pull that off? Did I think I could act as if I were voluntarily giving my breast for the nurturance of All of Our Relations? No, I did not think so, but I was going to try anyway.

Before dawn that morning, after dressing all in white, Adam and I went up into the park to meet the others.

It was an exceptionally clear and beautiful morning. The moon was approximating full and was setting as we climbed the hill. We all had instruments and items for an altar and offerings. It was about a ten-minute walk in the dark. As we set up the altar and put down our instruments, the sun was beginning to rise. I asked that the men accompany me to the point in the path where both mountains were visible and we stopped there, just off the path.

I asked that the men lower me on my stomach to the ground. I lay there for a few moments feelings my breasts against the earth. Then I rose to my knees and said vows that resembled wedding vows to the earth and to All of Our Relations. I said, "With this breast I thee wed—take this breast as a token of my love." I cried tears of joy as I recited these vows.

The men helped me back up and then went back to the altar site while I stayed to watch the sun come up over the north shoulder of Mount Diablo. I prayed and played my didge. The earth around me was alive in a way it never had been before. The bees, the birds, the tree, the grasses, the mountains, and the spaces between all of these were part of my family. I had made a promise to them all.

When I came back to the altar and the people, we had a celebration. No more funeral! And I actually felt like celebrating. The men and Elenna who participated in that ritual have never stopped thanking me for asking them to be part of it. I believe it changed all of us.

We took everyone out for breakfast and then I went off to have a massage with Joan Marie Passalacqua[2]. I still had on my white clothes when I arrived there, and she immediately sensed that this session would be beyond the ordinary. After I described where I had just come from, she lit candles and burned sage and readied me for the table.

What happened then is impossible to convey because I don't even know what happened, but I do know that she was speaking to the cells of my body, readying them for the surgery. She spoke to the cells in the body as the ritual had spoken to my psyche. She reassured them, and told them that no matter what, it would be okay, a blessing to all beings everywhere. She said goodbye on my behalf to my breast, and she let the cells say goodbye, too.

It was a requiem but not a funeral, an honoring but not morose. I burst out in tears partway through because it was so astonishingly beautiful. All was as it should be.

What was to be a fifteen minute session became over an hour, though I actually have no idea how much

2   See www.AppliedAnatomyInstitute.com (510) 843-2270.

time it took. It was outside time, much like when the ladder descended and called me on this journey. When I asked her how it felt to offer this gift, she just shrugged and said, "I kept being told to do something more and so I did."

At no time was I more convinced that this was an initiation. It was so clear that I was being asked to make a commitment to something larger than myself. On that day, I believed it. I still believe it. On that day, and the ones to follow, I became a believer in the power of ritual to actually alter the psyche and body—not to put one into denial of anything, but to shift at a cellular level the way one participates in what life offers.

Later in the day I had to drop something off at Elenna's where Mandaza was staying. At that moment he happened to be taking a break from private sessions; he played a special song on the mbira for me. The mbira is an instrument from Zimbabwe that is a a thumb piano inside a gourd. Mandaza plays it more sweetly than I have ever heard it played. His song stayed with me for a long time; maybe it is still with me today. I love mbira music as it seems to make my cells dance. I play a CD of that music when I am depressed or needing to heal because every note creates a corresponding bounce of resilience in my body.

I sent out an e-mail letting people know the time of my surgery the next day and asking for prayers.

❧

Sept.ember 3
Dear Friends and Family,
        My surgery has been scheduled for Friday at 8:00 a.m. I would love it if you would hold me in your prayers and if you are so inclined, ask for a couple of specific things:

1. My surgeon's name is Dr. V S and each time I have seen her, she is in a big hurry. I have asked her that before she makes a cut and before she sews me up, she please take a deep breath and think of healing and of beauty. So if you could hold those thoughts for her and for all of the other workers in the operating room, I would appreciate it. I sent her the Rumi quote: "Let the beauty you love be what you do; there are thousands of ways to kneel and kiss the earth."

2. I have gone through many transformations during the initiatory process of preparing for this surgery. I have come to the point now where I believe that it is a unique honor I have been given to offer this breast for the sake of healing and as nurturance for All Our Relations. I pray that I come through this as a more honed instrument of healing.

If you are on this list, you will be notified tomorrow of how surgery went and will get periodic updates. Thank you all for the support and love you have already given me. I take strength and courage from it.

Love,
Elise

&

I played self-hypnosis tapes that night before going to bed so that I would keep a positive thought about surgery and to let my body know again what was coming and how I was counting on it to recover well.

The next morning we woke very early. When I went to open the gate to the driveway, the full moon was shining down on me. I revelled there for a minute, thankful.

I took my didgeridoo with me to the hospital so that I could calm myself down if I got anxious.

We were a little late getting there and were one of the last people called to go into the private waiting rooms.

There was one other family in the waiting room. The thirteen-year-old boy was going in for mouth surgery. The father was sitting in the waiting room reading a book on how to quell anxiety, and he started talking to Adam about anxiety. So I took out the didge and asked if they minded if I played for a while, that it was really a good way to ease anxiety. They had no problem with it so I began by calling in the directions in my usual way. The last direction is space and unconditional love and for that I usually play a blessing song based on Eve Decker's song, "Lovingkindness."[3] I was moved to ask the boy if he minded if I played a blessing toward his heart. He agreed and I played the blessing for him. It calmed both of us.

Later in the private waiting room I played again because I started to get anxious. A variety of people came in and out, and they took into stride what I was doing. I cannot play the didge and be anxious. It just doesn't work. Circular breathing requires diaphramatic breathing and that itself cures anxiety.

I brought an mbira CD with me and handed that to the surgeon. I had sent her the e-mail referred to above and now she assured me that she would not be in a hurry. There was no CD player in the operating room but she was resourceful enough to use the laptop. The mbira was bouncing along when I went off under the anesthesia, having done all I could to prepare.

---

3   A song From Eve Decker's CD called *Commentaries on the Ten Perfections of the Heart*. See www.evedecker.com

CHAPTER FIVE

The Offering

The most unpleasant thing about the surgery was waking up in the recovery room. I was groggy and teary, and there was no one there who had any time to spend with me. It was, after all, the day before Labor Day weekend.

Workers were in a great rush to get me out of there and, though I had been told before the surgery that they would keep me there for a few hours and then decide whether I needed to stay overnight, this was not what happened. As soon as I was conscious, they were rushing to get me out the door. My husband, under the impression that I would be in there longer, was nowhere to be found. I didn't even have the $5.00 I needed to get the pain medicine; the nurse offered to lend it to me to get me out of there faster.

They had put a drain in the wound and the nurse started instructing me on how to empty it, but I was so groggy I could not to understand her at all. I asked if she could just wait for my husband to tell him. But she had no intention of waiting, and instead shoved a sheet of information into my hands. I remember when she said I could take the bandage off that night, I freaked out. I didn't know if I wanted to take it off—I didn't want to see it at all, ever!

Why did this happen; was it somehow outside the healing field? I don't know, but this kind of thing seemed to happen when I was perceived as just a body. Something about being just a slab of meat without consciousness. Maybe when I was not strong enough to stay aware and connected and there was no one who was doing it for me, the whole thing could turn sour.

The two times I had this feeling were the surgery pre-appointment and the recovery room. Maybe it was something about the mechanistic way a cold medical institution functions. The field seemed full of quotas, deadlines, numbers instead of healing, and I was unable to sway that for whatever reason. Once I was out of the hospital and with loved ones, I could regain a sense of the healing field.

This incident contrasts with the lumpectomy where Elenna was present, and even though I felt the cut, I did not feel abandoned. The cut happened. Then it was over, and I was done with it.

But in the recovery room, I felt no such connection or kindness, and I made no connection with anyone. The hurry-up energy was everywhere with many patients coming through and limited space and time. That, added to the fact that I was weak and unable to stay connected by myself, created a dismal re-entry.

The nurse got me dressed, though I am not sure how, and wheeled me over to another part of the recovery room to get me out of the way.

I had to start making calls to see if someone could come and pick me up since I couldn't find my husband. Friends who came to find out how I was were strong-armed into taking me home. Before they got me out of there, though, my husband showed up. I wished I had been spared that nightmarish awakening.

But I was so glad to be home. I had many e-mails waiting from people wishing me well which returned me to the healing field and brought my spirits back up.

Here are most of the e-mails that came in that day to give a feel for how it was that I came back into alignment with healing.

∾

Hi Elise,
Everyone I see asks about you so you have lots of people thinking and praying for you. You will certainly be in my prayers. love you lots.
Mom

∾

Hi Elise, know that my prayers have been with you and Dr. S this morning and will be through-out the day. May the surgery go well, and your recovery be quick so that you can get back to get back to what makes you you ....love you,
liz

∾

I am thinking of you and the bravery you have demonstrated to all of us. I was home alone (Cynthia's home) last night had some time to send you some music. At six AM I sent out your prayer to the doctor. You are loved, as always I offer my help.
Viviane

∾

I am with you, Elise, in spirit. The piece that follows ["Night Chant, a Navajo Poem" (as recorded by Eduardo Galeano in his Memory of Fire Trilogy) is not written by me, but it seems to belong in this chain of intentions for beauty and healing. You may already know it.
Jane

❧

It's 9 am on Sept. 4, I am with you and V and All Our Relations.
Love, Joya

❧

Dear Elise,
I received this just after 8 am on the 4th, today, and started in particular sending you support and love, and for your surgeon gentle support for her breathed intent. You are so held in a circle of love and of loving friends. I will especially think of you in the next while during your surgery, sending you love and fellowship, and yes, what a tender offering of your breast for nurturing for all our relations...may it be so, and may you feel and know the tender holding and space of healing and love around you.
blessings and hugs,
Cress

❧

Dearest Elise,
You are so dearly and tenderly in my heart since you have shared your journey. I especially send you my deepest healing prayers and love and also to Dr. S as she opens the flesh that protects your heart. May she find a moment of prayer in herself and hold silence. May your offering nurture all beings.
I am so there with you in Spirit.
Love, Prayer and healing,
Dipti

❧

Hello dear friend, I just wanted to let you know that I am thinking about you on a daily basis. Alicia is lighting candles for you and will contact you at some point—when you are ready. I will call you next week—after you have had some time to recoup.

Lots of love...Donna

❧

Dear Elise,

I am thinking of you as this late night is about to become tomorrow's morning. And I am holding you in my thoughts and prayers. You will be surrounded by many loving spirits when you are in your surgery and your doctor will feel their impact, and the impact of the words you wrote to her. I look forward to seeing you on the other side of this and to being there, in whatever way you need, to help you heal.

Love to you,
Juli

❧

Dear Elise,

Dr. S was also my friend and co-worker's wife's doctor. He said she was a very caring doctor.

I am praying for healing and beauty for V and for you.

With Aloha,
Joan

❧

I will be holding you in thoughts and prayers.

With love, Brenda

❧

Sending a lot of love, light, beauty and breath to you and the surgeon and pray for the healing of all our relations.

With love, Nicki

❧

I am holding the globe of the moon in my deep
self
I am holding your honored presence in the deep
self
I am holding your blessed self in my deep self
I am holding your gift to the world in the deep
self
I am holding you
I am holding you
I am holding you my friend.

All Love, Meg

ps: the moon waxes into full tomorrow am - good
sign—the mother of all is holding you.

❧

I will be thinking of you Elise, and your surgeon. I will be thinking of your bravery and
your generosity and love for others.
Linda

❧

Dear Elise,
I will be holding your intentions in my
prayers. Please, count on that.
With much love for your healing process,
Susana

❧

Dear Elise,
You have been in my thoughts all day, all
week, all month.

Healing energy,
Loving compassion,
Brave courage,
Selfless giving.

These are yours,
They surround you,
They are within you,
They resonate with your beauty.

I, and we, your Daré community,
Hold you in our hearts.
The circle is unbroken.
    Blessing to you, dear One,
    BaBaruce

❧

Ash`e! Ah`o!
much love and light,
    OwlSnake

Elise,
    We are and will be thinking of you. We want
you back, safe and sound, and expect nothing
less. Go for it!
    Mark

❧

Dearest Elise,
    I was just praying for you this morning. You
offer yourself up to God so eloquently. I'm moved
by your raw truth. Thank you for sharing this
most intimate part of your newly born spirit-
self.
    Gail

❧

    Elise, no sweat that you didn't call me back.
I can imagine how things are for you right now.
Just want you to know that I am here for you in
whatever way you feel you need, given my limi-
tations. I sure can talk to you about what it is
like, give you any good tips that I learned, like
taking 200 arnica for the surgery trauma/pain.
I don't do well on narcotics, so I took arnica the
morning of the surgery, and as late as I could
before going under, then again as soon as I
could in recovery, then for the next day or so.
I really had very little if any pain. I more felt
sadness, I cried, I talked a lot coming out of the
anesthesia, but I wasn't in pain. So, you might

want to try some. I am not sure where you can get it now that Elephant Pharmacy is closed. If I have some I will bring it to you. I have to look for it, our house is turned upside down.

Being in silence is good preparation for the surgery. The worst part of all is the waiting. All the waiting for this and for that. So, be prepared.

Love and abrazos to you, talk to you soon.
XXX Suzie

❧

Elise,
I'll keep you in my thoughts on Friday. We've got a lot more music together ahead.
Sincerely,
Phil

❧

Dear Elise
I feel honored to pray for you and your doctor and your breast. I know that your spirit will sing and play the didge and all will be well in healing and beauty. Big Hug and kiss!
Love, Pemba

❧

Dear Elise,
I will be holding you in my mind/heart tomorrow. I hope you can let us know the time so we can target our intentions. I love you and am praying for your health.
Love, Joyce

❧

September 4 (sent to the e-mail list)
Hi Everyone,

I just heard from Elise. She's back home. Her voice sounded strong and she seems to be in good spirits. The doctors expect a fast recovery and she will be able to do light or normal things tomorrow although she won't be able to drive due to the meds she needs. She's going to take a nap right now so it's probably best not to call her;

however, she welcomes your e-mails. Also, she's planning to send an e-mail to all of you once she's recovered a bit more and will let you know when it's okay to call and if she has any requests. Adam's doing okay too, but could probably use some TLC after all he and Elise have been through.

Elise brought her didge to the hospital and played for a young man, who was also awaiting surgery, to help calm his anxious family. She then played for herself in the waiting room.

Love,   Joyce (Rybandt)

꙰

Dear Elise,

I'm glad to hear you got through the operation and that you're recovering pretty well. I'm sending you lots of healing energy and love. It must be a huge adjustment and I know that your strength and bravery will shine forth. I hope you are feeling the big circle of loving supportive women who were around you for the ritual and still are there. I will be out of town until Thursday, after that let me know if there is anything I can do.

Love Brigid

꙰

Dear Elise,

I was thinking about you the whole time I was sitting in the dentist chair today, from 8 - 9:30 a.m. Since you got home so early I guess it went smoothly and on time. Good. And good for you to be playing your didge and helping someone else.

You seem to have a good handle spiritually on how to respond to this cancer, and I applaud you. This will be a hard journey, so please know that we all are your angels right now and are hovering over you to keep you safe. Call me any time,

Love and abrazos,
Suzie

๛

Dear Elise;
  My prayers will continue for your speedy recovery.
  Sending you Love and light.
  Bola

๛

Dear Elise,
  You are an inspiration. I love it that you played your didge for yourself and others before going into surgery.
  I am very happy that you are doing so well.
  As with everyone else, know that my thoughts and love and prayers are coming your way. I look forward to more updates.
  Two Hands Together,
  Brenda

๛

You know the Sufi symbol of a heart with wings. I see a breast with wings. I Love You!,
  joya

๛

Dear Friends and Family,

It is the day after surgery and I feel so lucky to have been released yesterday to have a relaxing day and night at home instead of, well, you know how hospitals are, especially on a holiday weekend.

I am having very little pain, just when I try to make certain moves but not overall generalized pain which I am thankful for.

I looked at the scar this morning and it is quite long and very straight. It reminds me of a good long lifeline on a palm of one's hand.

As for prayers which I hope you all can continue to send.... I have gone through many transformations during this initiatory process of preparing for this surgery. I have come to the point now where I believe that it is a unique honor I have been given to offer this breast for the sake of healing and as nurturance for All of Our Relations. I

continue to pray that I come through this as a more honed instru-
ment of healing.
    Sending out love,
    Elise

❧

My friend Lucy had offered to come over anytime I needed help, and Adam asked if she could come that first day after surgery since he wanted to go to his poetry group meeting. The Bay Bridge was closed that weekend for major road work and, even so, Lucy who lives in the City agreed to come. She had to come by way of two bridges.

By the time she got there, I had started worrying about why the scar was so long. The place where it was hurting the most was under the arm. We measured it to be ten inches long. I hadn't been able to talk to the surgeon after the surgery and neither had anyone else. A doctor who had assisted in the surgery stopped by when I was still groggy. I wondered if perhaps there had been something unexpected that they had had to remove. I tried to call my surgeon while Lucy was there, but she didn't answer.

I called Elenna and got unreasonably angry with her because she had not talked to the surgeon after the surgery. Elenna tried calling Dipti, who had been through this herself, but we couldn't get through to her until later that day. By doing some healing work with me, singing to me and having me write collaborative poems with her, Lucy was able to calm me down.

Later that evening Dipti assured me that it is not unusual for the scar to be very long and that breast tissue goes all the way under the arm. After that conversation I was fine.

Here are more e-mails that are representative of what I received.

❧

such a life—such love such care
from you for all
which is yourself
your chest the palm of heart
your scarred blessing marks the place
of courage—sussurus' meter

small hammer and anvil in the chest
your lifeline giving—giving love.

love, meg

❧

Dear Elise,
You will come through this with a deep sense of knowing, understanding, and purpose. You are becoming a finely tuned, unique and beautiful instrument of healing. It is an honor to witness... and a privilege to walk the path with you.
With love,
~Karen

❧

yesterday in honor of you I went to our sacred spots to send you prayers. I visited Goat Rock, waded in the Russian river, walked through a forest hoping to send you a breath of fresh air from the sea, river and the trees. I prayed and sang that you would feel peace...
your friend Viviane

❧

Hi Elise—
Congratulations on a successful and speedy operation, and home sweet home. I am so moved by how you approached all this—I will remember it always and it will help me when my inevitable health challenges come up.

I'll be waiting to bring you soup, massage or whatever TLC either you or Adam need—We'll sing for you at Womansong[1]! If you are up and around, it would be wonderful to have you in the circle, sing right to/into you, bring the healing music right into your body direct!

Love, Betsy

❧

Dear Elise,

how moved I feel by these e-mails you've sent, and by the wisdom—hard won—that you bring and share. You help me to reflect, to perceive, to feel beyond the boundaries of the fearful ways that I too often shrink to, and into such openings to life and living in its so many varied ways. Thank you for the beauty you bring.

You are so in my thoughts, and prayers. I hear such music when I tune to you, and have the sense of such love and support around and through you.

Blessings,
Cress

❧

You have been in my heart since our talk...I am glad to know you are home and on your continued self healing journey. I will hold on the visit as I know many people will be visiting — but know that you can call or e-mail anytime.

Love and light,
Saundra

❧

Dear Elise,

I am so happy to hear that you are doing so well. I continue to send you lots of love and healing energy. I was in Kaiser yesterday morning getting blood tests and was sending energy up your way through the building.

Much love, Alexis

---

1   See www.BetsyRoseMusic.org.

❧

Hi Elise:

I spent yesterday morning listening to Mozart and sending love and healing your way… I had told Susan what was up, and she had to teach yesterday morning so at five minutes to eight yesterday, right before the instructors went to teach classes, Susan walked out into the hall, summoned them all, got them in a circle holding hands, and they sent prayers and love to you. I was so touched. She is the most wonderful person, and I am blessed to have the both of you for friends.

Love and Healing and Light,
Meg & Susan

❧

Yay you're home. So is your lovely breast. She's gently rockin' humanity awake.

Love, joya

❧

Dear Elise,

I am so glad it went smoothly, and that you are resting… It does not surprise me that you would be offering help and support to another as you wait for surgery yourself. Thank you for your sacrifice and prayers on behalf of the motherline, and for your grace and humanity…

love, pamela

❧

September 7
Dear all,

Today it has been occurring to me that I have shape-shifted. Not knowing just what that means, I went online to see if I could make meaning out of it. I found the following quote which seemed meaningful to me, having just gone through this painful experience.

"'You have lost touch with the Mother,' he said. He stood up, held out his arms, and turned in a slow circle. He clenched his hands into fists and drew them to his heart. 'Now it begins to hurt....I sometimes think that all we care about is money and dominating things. Other people, other countries. Nature. That we've lost the ability to love.'

His eyes met mine, a stern look. 'You haven't lost the ability.'"
—Numi, Shuar Shaman

And I know, indeed, that we have not lost the ability to love—I see it in the responses I am getting back regarding my notes about the surgery and preparation for it. Let's move it from ability to action wherever we can.

I am well today, adjusting to my shape-shifted body and spirit. The whole experience feels like one huge teaching. I have done none of it by myself, but have been handed lesson after lesson and have simply opened my hand and heart and received—from friends, from nature, from community, from the long dark night, from ancestors, from places and spirits I had not previously been to or met.

Can a person who has been through this sort of thing really feel as blessed as I feel? The journey continues.

Keep sending love out,
Elise

❧

Elise, you are so precious...I just feel like anything I have to say right now would seem trite, given the depth of what you are feeling and experiencing with the loss that has been turned into a spiritual experience.
I love you, Donna.

❧

Elise,
Loveloveloveloveloveloveloveloveiamstillvibratingfromplayingthedidgeforyouyesterday-loveloveloveloveloveloveiamstillvi-
love,
Alan

❧

May your recovery process be gentle . . .
May you heal throughout your being . . .
May all beings be free from suffering . . .
Namaste, Yolanda

❧

Dearest Elise,
    Yes it is possible to feel blessed after an experience such as this. I do ... I have come to feel both blessed and grateful ... something I knew I would eventually feel, yet struggled with shortly after my own shape-shifting. This is the piece I wrote at the time. I extend it as an offering for you now.
    Sending love,
    ~Karen

SOMEDAY I'LL BE GRATEFUL
By Karen Jandorf

If you touch my chest, you will feel my heart in your hand.
It is that close to the surface.
All its protective covering has been taken away.

If you hug me, you will feel my heart beat against your chest.
You will know the syncopation of my fear, my excitement, my equanimity.
There is no camouflage left.

If you see me, you will notice my shoulders fighting.
Curling inward, stretching outward.
Conflicting desires to contract and expand.

If you sense me, you will feel my heart protecting itself.
It is too naked, too raw, too vulnerable.
Energetic armor created in the wake of exposure.

If you love me, though, you will invite me to unfold.
Your hand will become a safe haven for my broken-winged heart.
You will slowly and gently help me remove the suit of arms.
Your heart will become my polyrhythm and you will dance with me.

CHAPTER SIX

Notes from the Healing Frontier

On Friday, September 11, I had the drain removed from the wound. Adam drove me there and it was my first time outside my neighborhood. The doctor said the wound looked fine and dismissed me as a patient. I was given a couple of camisoles that had a pocket to stuff so that I could look at least somewhat symmetrical as I made my way in the world. They were a comfort to me.

That would be the last time I saw anyone in that clinic.

The original schedule I had for the Sound, Voice and Music Healing class showed it starting on September 19, two weeks after surgery. But they revised the schedule, setting the first class for September 12. Since that was only one week and a day after surgery, I knew attending it would be pushing my limits. Sarah from Daré came along with me to drive me there and keep an eye on me. I had told the administration about my situation but just as the director of the program had not read my e-mail of explanation, no one seemed to have any idea of the tender and vulnerable state I was in.

Later, I talked to someone in the class who had noticed me and, though she didn't know me, wondered if I was well because I looked so white. I made it through until about 2:30 p.m. and then had to leave. The last thing I participated in was when each of us sang out our names and where we were from with some kind of gesture. I did it, but it took everything I had.

Alexis from Daré came by to give me cranial-sacral work. She worked primarily on my arm which was still so injured and getting worse since I was holding my arm so strangely. Right after the surgery when I noticed myself in a mirror, my right shoulder was up in the air, much higher than the left one.

Alexis did the body work and gave me some oils to use in the healing process. That session helped me to be more in touch with my poor arm and to give it what it needed. I appreciated Alexis' work with me so much that day; she came to me and brought healing.

Alan, a didgeridoo student of mine, and Daré member, began coming twice a week to play the didge for me. This turned out to be a great way for him to practice sustained circular breathing, and he did it so well. Sometimes he seemed to go into an altered state, and once he played continuously for an hour. I so appreciated that faithfulness and generosity of spirit, not to mention the healing effects.

I had a dream on September 14 that Lucy's friend was dying. In the dream, *Lucy (or someone else) has a dream in which she is told to get water from a deep well. The dreamer*

*thinks that the water is for the dying friend but I tell her that
the friend is already dead, and the water is for her. I wonder in
the dream how Lucy can spend so much time with me when her
friend is dying. The friend's name is that of a goddess, something
very familiar to me but with a twist at the end.*

In some ways Lucy's friend, Elise, had died. I was not
the same as I had been before. Some part of me had died
through this process. Before the surgery, the only plans
that I made for the self I would be after the surgery was
the Sound Healing class. Otherwise, I had no idea who I
would be. I wanted to leave it that way.

❧

September 15
Dear loved ones,

*I wanted to let you know that I have had the drain removed
from my wound and am now feeling more human again. I almost said
more "normal" but I can't find normal yet and maybe don't want to
find it. My right arm still has mobility problems, a lot of tightness and
some pain. My energy is slowly returning but I have to watch how
much I attempt to do in one day or one period of time without resting.*

*I was talking to a friend the other day and told her that I
am inclined lately to start crying at the drop of a hat and that once
crying, I am very close to sobbing. She was surprised because my e-
mails have sounded so positive. She thought I must have been leaving
out the bad stuff. Right now I am not seeing things as bad and good.
Instead, the place I am living in at the moment seems less narrow, not
one that seeks "positive" and shuns "negative" but one in which all of
it exists simultaneously with no labels.*

*I feel as if the horizon has expanded, leaving spaciousness for
whatever is arising in the moment. If it is sobbing, I can name that as
grief for what is lost, (and that is not just a breast, but all the precious*

beings and things that we have all lost, individually and collectively). If it is clarity that arises, I find it is not the kind of clarity I am used to, that is, a clarity about right and wrong or what I like or don't like, want or don't want. This clarity contains no judgment; it is merely a witness, seeing sharply and clearly a larger picture than before.

One of the characters in the new movie Taking Woodstock says something like, "It's all of these little perspectives that people have that get in the way of love." The little perspectives that show us what we deem good and bad have little to do with the big picture, with the landscape.

My own landscape has changed; a new epoch has begun. This newly carved plain and this path etched across my chest serves as a clarion call, a wake up to awareness. The sight of it, the feel of it, is still a shock, a visceral way to remember that something has changed, that I cannot go back to business as usual.

If I do not seem like the person I was before this physical and psychic shift, it is because I am not. Just who I am now is as yet undefined and still shaping herself. This part involves all of you and all of our relations. Who I am has so much to do with who we are together as we reweave our relationships with love.

This state of being feels like such a gift. I am grateful for it and relishing every moment. May I not get back to normal anytime soon!

Love,
Elise

❧

September 15: Deena Metzger's response
Elise dear:

I am writing to you from Manhattan. A few minutes ago, I was involved in a small miracle... . [She detailed an incident for me where she ran into someone from the past by "accident" on the streets of Manhattan.]

I was able to reflect with her on her life. It had tragedy in it and she had experienced so much illness. But she is alive. And the miracle of that became obvious in our little exchange. "Why has Spirit continuously given you the miracle of life?," I asked her, "What gift is Spirit calling forth from you? Why these miracles?"

A miracle. An event choreographed exactly for a divine purpose we can't imagine, but we must acknowledge, —

And so...

Here you are cataloguing the small changes in your situation that will lead to a change in consciousness we can't imagine, but must acknowledge.

I am so glad you are recovering — it happens slowly — the surgery simple as it is, or so they say, is also a big deal and it takes time to recover, enough time for us to develop the consciousness we need to develop so that we don't go back to the old life which we would if we healed immediately.

You are also reminding me of all the times I cried in restaurants, after surgery. It always surprised me. I would be in a conversation, someone said something, and I would be bawling. I don't bawl. I didn't bawl then. But during the weeks or months after surgery, I did.

May you gain strength and insight in partnership.

Bless you,
Deena

❧

Ahhhh! "There is a field out beyond right and wrong. I will meet you there." Rumi.

Love, Meg

❧

Dear Elise,

I am so touched by what you write, by your aliveness with all of this. I have sometimes felt cracked open—by losses, or being touched

by something so vast, and have wept, sobbed,
howled. Sometimes those near me have worried
or tried to make this go away as if it were a bad
thing, and for me too, it really isn't ever a question of good or bad, though I would say there is
a goodness in just letting myself be so, letting it
flood through me, or me flood. Then what com-
forts me most (though it often isn't a question of
comfort being wanted even) is being with people
who can just sit with me as the time passes, and
not try and word it or make it go away, but just
bear (as carry) it with me.

I have been thinking of you such a lot lately,
and yet not known what to say so stayed silent,
but you are so in my thoughts and heart.
    with love,
    Cress

❧

Dear Elise and Deena,
    All of your words, tears, and unexplainable
meetings are the way of life as we have been
asked to offer the flesh that protects our hearts. I
am so deeply touched with the love and wisdom
you have offered here.
    Thank you.
    Love,
    Dipti

❧

    Aaaw yes my friend, you are not only shifting
physically more importantly spiritually. I soooo
know the crying at the drop, headed towards
sobbing. You have reached the level of your
initiation where you feel the world...outside of
yourself. Yes I am sure there may still be the grief
you may feel of your sacrifice, but when I read
this I was given an image of myself wailing like
i sometimes do for no apparent reason, but to
shed tears for the sorrows of the world. As vessels
for Spirit to utilize to heal the world (one at a

time), it is the way.
   much love and light,
   OwlSnake

❧

Dear Elise~
   Thank you for continuing to share this
amazing unfolding of life's journey for you.
The opening to all emotions, the spaciousness
you experience to all aspects, is a heart-opening
reminder to me of moments in my life where a
great shock/crisis/loss has split me open, opened
my consciousness to a much wider plane, (a mis-
carriage comes strongly to memory) and even
as I was suffering, I felt such gratitude for the
direct tapping into my humanity and my spiri-
tuality, my /our divinity. In a way, this is what
we live for—moments/times that plunge us into
the real stuff of living, interrupt the trance of
"normal" life. The Zen knock on the head, Buddha underneath the Boddhi tree...
   with much love—and awe—
   Betsy

❧

Thank you for writing Elise.
   I had skin cancer roughly four or five years
ago (the scar on my neck)... Even though it was
a minor procedure, I can attest that surgery is
traumatic. Particularly the realization that
something was being cut out of me, part of me
was now gone, but a part that was damaging
myself. In some ways, I still feel the scar, that
strange sense of closure on my neck.
   It's funny Deena wrote while I was writing
you, she has a quote that resonated with me
as well:
         "Did you think The Presence
          would fail to leave a scar?"
   Sincerely,
   Phil

❧

Dear Elise,

I was sitting here at the computer when this e-mail came from you. What you are describing is what I (and probably all others on the spiritual path) yearn, or have yearned for, always. To see things clearly, without judgment, without prejudice, just simply to see what is. To have the capacity to be an observer; that is a muscle I try to develop, completely forget about, then am reminded by such things as your writing today.

I have been feeling very depressed the last few weeks; not clinically, but just a feeling of loss. I think for me, it's about the state of our country and how we have lost our old ideals and the idea of working together in communities to help one another. I didn't think I would live to see "My Country" devolve to this.

I now realize that it is up to me to clear up my own state of being, that I can't just be pained that other people are acting in certain ways that I don't like. I need to see the larger picture that includes everything and everyone.

Thank you for this e-mail. I hope that you will not feel you have to be any certain way with your friends (I count myself among them.)

You do not have to be anything except Elise, in whatever shape she/you take in any given moment. Normal is not a place you want to be... unless you happen to be there. Acceptance, it always comes back to that!

Love to you,
Juli

❧

Hi Elise,

Much love and thank for sharing your beautiful, expansive process with all of us. I feel like I am growing with you.

XO Alexis

❧

Dear Elise,

I also hope you do not go back to "normal," as I also know that I will not. Your writing and ability to be spacious is beautiful. It is a gift to all of us. The landscape changes and we are witness to it.

May all love continue to surround you.
Brenda

❧

Elise,

I have just stated to receive your e-mails via Mark. The address that you had for me is very old and you will need to add my current e-mail address to your list.

What you are saying in your e-mails is not something that I can yet get my arms around. I need time to adjust to the new reality and to fully digest what you are writing. That is not to suggest that I will not be able to do this - I think I always have a connection to you and are able to understand that which I take the time to digest. I will read and reread these and come to understand where you are right now.

On a simpler note, I hope that you are healing well and that your strength comes back soon. I am sure that it will. It seems that your perspective may be forever changed, and that is often a great gift.

Please add me to your e-mail list.
Your loving brother,
Jim

❧

On September 18, two weeks after surgery, I returned to the Y to swim. I wanted all the support I could get and was lining that up as best I could. At the last minute, my regular swimming partner could not come, but as usual through this ordeal, my stalwart Elenna was there for me. I

had a bathing suit that my daughter-sister Pemba had gotten me, and I had a silicone breast to fit into the pocket
that was given to me by my sister Sue It was a little bit big
but unless one looked closely, that was unnoticeable. Getting me back in the water had been a team effort.

That first day, I noticed that I was edgy and a little
uncertain of myself but ready to go forward. I found a locker in the row that did not have a mirror at the end of it and
I went to the end of the row so that my right side faced
the wall. Someone had suggested that I dress before coming to the Y and that way, no one would see me. That idea
just made me angry. For me—and this is not to judge anyone else who chooses a different way—if I am hiding, I feel
ashamed of myself. And if I do that, the game is over and I
have lost. If I give in to my own tendency to want to hide, I
know it is a slippery slope into complete and utter avoid-
ance of all the hard issues of my life. I was a living metaphor,
and some part of me knew it. If I succumbed to hiding at
the Y, what is to keep me from hiding over and over again
in my life? This is not everyone's issue but I could see that
it was mine.

This surgery was no gentle nod to tell me I was
already doing everything right. No, this ordeal showed me
exactly where I needed to make changes and work toward
not slipping back to who I had been before the surgery.
Perhaps my true self was no different, but how I walked in
the world with that truth was hopefully forever changed.

I was worried that the false breast would escape and
float away, or behave strangely in the water. But it did fine
and so did I. Here I was exactly two weeks after surgery,

back in the water. I was so proud of myself. I could hardly use my right arm at all but I worked around that. Ironically enough, I seemed to be able to do the breast stroke very well.

ॐ

September 19
Dear Loved Ones,

Notes from the Healing Frontier

With another week behind me in this healing journey, I feel as if I have moved from private healing sphere into a more public one. I am back in public spaces: plays, concerts, teaching didge class, classes for my Sound Healing certificate program, and I started swimming again last Friday.

Now different issues arise. I run into acquaintances who know nothing of this surgery and I wonder what to do. They ask how I am. The first time, not wanting to hide, I told the person that I had had a mastectomy. But that didn't work out well. The person was taken aback, horrified, sympathetic—none of those things felt connected in the present moment to me. I felt as if there was no way to tell her about it without telling her the whole thing and how, though there are horrible aspects, it has been a gift. But often in the public sphere there is no time for that. I decided not to do that again but to simply say that I am well—which incidentally, I am.

And at the Y it hasn't taken me long to give up the idea of completely hiding myself—it is just too much trouble. So in that place if someone glimpses me, I am visualizing myself as art where, if the art piece draws a gasp, that is good—it means that viewers have been viscerally reached, startled into different places that shifted their thinking in some way. I began picturing my body as something Picasso might paint. Here is a quote of his I like: "The purpose of art is washing the dust of daily life off our souls." Maybe my body can do that for me as well as for others.

I noticed this morning that the scar is not stationary; the path which at rest has a slight incline of maybe 5 degrees from left to right, can move up to a 15 or 20 degree incline when I raise up my arm. I'm not sure why this is meaningful, but somehow it makes the whole thing more alive, not static nor stagnant. So fist raised into the air, I say for all of us, "The journey lives. Long live the journey!"

Open to Guidance,
Elise

೬

Dear Elise,
  I think that when you raise your arm your scar is trying to smile! What else could it do when it is residing in such a positive artist's body!
  Love, Pemba

೬

E: Your scar, like you, has many tangents, many entrance points into the dialog with life and death. I imagine an arrow pointing the way, and then a weathervane that shifts and goes with a sudden change in the wind direction, the loose and relaxed way in which your change of physical aspect has completely driven the weathervane of focus for you and many of the rest of us. Interesting how whatever you write about this seems to find its way into some sort of magical imagery for me. I move from tall, glass buildings to a seagull over choppy water, to the blue/purple of mountains, and then a patch of green in the middle of a tarmac surface.
  Thanks, and I love you.
  Meg

೬

hi elise,
  my friend you are a living example of possibilities. much love and light, OwlSnake

೬

Thanks so much for sending me Elise's Post-surgery blog. It was inspiring for the bigness of soul and depth of honesty. Give her my best.

Kindest regards,
Malcolm

❧

Dear Elise,
Thank you for including me in your healing blog, I am much honored. You are certainly giving me insight and support to go through any future and current difficulties. And I want to say in response to your last letter.... I love you Elise.

Love,
Joan

❧

Dear Adam and Elise,
Thank you both for sharing this with us. It's one of the most honest and deeply moving testaments I've ever seen from someone facing cancer and surgery. I don't know whether I would be able to be both so honest and so brave, but I will keep this in my heart and mind and go back to it in the future if the time ever comes. It's a great gift to everyone who gets to read it.

Love,
Ken and Linda

❧

On September 22, I went to the second Sound Healing class in San Francisco. We were taught by a psychotherapist who led us in a ritual that brought in our hopes and intentions for the class. In small groups, we were asked to tell the story of how we ended up in the Sound Healing class. I remember thinking, well, it's now or never—I might as well tell my story.

I told it rather dispassionately because by that time I *felt* rather dispassionate. I was not terribly sad or upset. In fact, I felt very good. I was feeling as if I had had an initiation and had gotten through it, and this class was gravy. Nothing could touch me. The others in the group, however, were moved by the story and amazed that I could be starting class at such a time. I had no idea how I would get through telling strangers my story. But I was fine and, in fact, felt a great relief that someone in the the class knew my story. Then I could relax. I could get on with learning about sound healing, something I felt I was already launched into, some-thing I was certainly prepared to do.

In the class, we were asked to bring a notebook to hold handouts and organize our notes. Onto the front of mine, I pasted a copy of a photograph of the altar I made from the plaster cast of my torso, with fresh flowers spring-ing out over the top. That way, each time I took out the notebook, I would be reminded of my initiation.

About six weeks after surgery, I made an appoint-ment to go to Nordstrom's to get a prosthesis and a bra. The fitting was a strange affair since I don't believe I have ever been in Nordstom's before, and I felt like a fish out of water. The clerk was very kind and patient and she did her best to make me look "normal."

Strangely enough the minute I left the store, my pe-riod started, so we had based my "normal" on a swollen breast and the prosthesis turned out to be too big. I rarely wear it anyway, preferring the lighter weight camisole or soft bra. I left feeling emotional and ungrounded. I was a little hard on myself, expecting that I should be able to handle this easily and not knowing why it upset me.

That clerk was the first stranger to see the scar, and it was her job to make sure that I would look normal. There is something off-putting to me about stores that specialize in making people want to look or to be different than they are. Again it brought up the issue of being ashamed of myself somehow.

Asymmetry is a hard thing to get used to and seems to draw attention to itself. I still needed to hide but was uncomfortable with the extent to which one would go to have something look "real." What is real anyway, the way I am, or the way I want people to see me? Calling all philosophers...

Sometimes I go around
pitying myself,

when all the while,
I am being carried by
great winds across the sky.
—Chippewa saying

CHAPTER SEVEN

Becoming a Healing Presence

In the early days of the Sound Healing class, I soaked up whatever the teachers said. I was listening deeply; I rarely spoke in the class, taking the opportunity to just listen to teachers and classmates alike. Teacher Pauline Oliveras, an expert on deep listening, urged us to play with the ideas of full spectrum listening; how to keep the background in one's consciousness as well as the foreground. And to learn to shift between the two.

Again the idea of focus arises. Where do I focus my attention? I find that just as I spoke of a camera zooming in and out, sounds similarly can be chaotic if you listen at one level. But if you can focus differently, the sounds can make a different kind of sense or be pleasing. Sounds bombard us constantly: talk radio, advertisements, music not of our choosing, machines. I began to practice resting in stillness and letting the sounds just be sounds and not bombardment, focusing on the space between the sounds without resisting what arises. I am improving at this, especially if I couple it with sitting quietly in nature and broadening my awareness to 360 degrees around me.[1]

I have often thought that listening was passive, but I realize now that what I thought of as passive is quite actively setting aside ego and the chattering mind. It takes vigilance. At silent retreats, I used to imagine that silence occurred when the humans stopped talking. That kind of silence only allows me to hear how present and loud the voices in my head are. Once I identify those voices, I can detach from them. They grow quieter. What is left is not empty but rather full of vibration. There I can find my own vibration and where it fits into the rest of nature.

My classmates in the sound healing class (or co-hearts, as we called each other) were an eclectic group from all walks of life. Some were scientists, body workers, musicians, activists, or a combination of those things. I savored just being part of this extraordinary class.

At the one-month mark after surgery, I could feel myself a different person, more alive, more present, more appreciative of life, without judgment of whether something was good or bad.

Elenna marked the occasion with an e-mail that had me in tears of resonance. This letter validated my experience and allowed me to move on, walking in a new way.

---

1   Concept from Jon Young, www.jonyoung.org.

Ȕ

October 2

> "Let the beauty you love be what you do;
> there are thousands of ways
> to kneel and kiss the earth."
> —Rumi

My dear Elise,

I sit here in bed with my eyes wet with tears, reading through every one of the notes you have sent out these 5 months since you discovered the mass in your breast.

It was the note to Dr. S that finally started me weeping. So I ask myself why that one of the many you wrote so devotedly during this time in your life, in our lives, in the life of the Daré—this community we both love, are sometimes exasperated by, and over whom we often collapse into tears of varying parts exasperation, humor and awe?

In your words to Dr. S, I could actually feel how wide you had thrown open your heart and arms through all of this. Feeling this melted me. You never once kept anyone outside of what you were experiencing. You "simply" required that each and every one who wanted to accompany you do so as nakedly, with as much awe and gratitude as you were mustering to walk through the unknown into a wholeness you could never have imagined awaited. There was something in how you scooped your surgeon up and brought her along, inviting her as we invited Dipti's surgeon Anne 5 years prior, to be not only a doctor but a healer.

Your words to Dr. S both acknowledged her world and called her into yours, into the one we can all share together in which beauty, breath, Self, self and community are redefined and remade over and over again. Thank you.

It was kind of funny when we realized that over all of these months I'd not once written in response to your raw and generous chronicle. While I read each of your notes—albeit in my own time—the arc of our connection unfolded, not surprisingly, in the realm of the body on walks at the marina, in too many Kaiser waiting rooms, on the dark night street in front of your house, in locker rooms and operating rooms, with you alone and as one among your community of men and women, the visible and invisible, the Ancestors reaching for you.

And still we agreed that we wanted something on paper, succumbing perhaps to the illusion of it being more real than memory? Whatever the reason, I am grateful to be revisiting what has transpired these last months, to ask just what do I want to say to you from "the other side"? This is what comes.

You have been impeccably real and naked to the bone with yourself and with us. In being so you have invited every one of us to experience courage and be completely exposed to ourselves, each other, to you and to Spirit. You have shown us how, when given the chance, a community can be essential to healing and transformation. You have shown us how a community is transformed by the journey of any one of its own. And through your wisdom in recognizing Spirit's irresistible call to surrender, we have been trained and blessed, honored to serve and become more than we knew ourselves to be before.

There has been joy in this journey, music and grace, honesty and a cascade of gifts that have fallen into all of our lives. Most vivid in this moment is Karen, who when called upon to accompany you through your fear of public exposure, seized the opportunity to turn a boundary into a threshold and become even more visible in her bare-chested beauty.

Finally, my dear sister, your authenticity, courage and wisdom have gifted me in ways I cannot yet express. Thank you for allowing, no trusting me, to accompany you on this journey. It has been such a privi-

*lege to be washed in your tears, stretched and enlight-
ened by your questions, collapsed in the laughter of
true surrender, and warmed by the feel of you moment
by moment more fully inhabiting the blessing of your
wisdom body.*

*Thank you for the healing you are. I love you
beyond words.*

*With two hands touching and tears of joy on my
cheeks, I bow to you.*

Elenna

∾

October 15
Dearest Community,

It has been five months today since I discovered that I had
a guest growing in my right breast and almost 7 weeks since I made
an offering of that breast for the nurturance of All of Our Relations. I
pause now to write you one last letter.

I have been swimming regularly since two weeks after surgery and my muscles seem to be returning, as is the feeling in the
incision area, (though I understand that is often not the case). I am
rather fond of my thin pink line as it shows up day after day in its
vulnerability, its infancy.

I would not be so fond of that thin pink line and may not
have felt free to go back to the Y without the support of all of you,
including Karen's breaking the ice for us as we went to the Y before
the surgery, step-daughter Pemba's buying me a swim suit, my sister
Sue getting a silicone breast to fit in the little pocket, Elenna's going
with me for the first time after the surgery, and Dipti's honest presence.

It took a community to keep me from feeling the shame
I was so sure I would feel after the surgery, yet have not. It took a
community willing to share every step, to respond with such love and
respect. Someone recently asked me if in sharing this, I did not open
myself up for yuckiness as well. I think she meant that I might evoke

pity, or horror, or unwanted advice. But with a few very minor exceptions, I can say that I did not get the yuckiness, just the knowledge that I was not alone, that people were here to listen and eager to help in any way they could.

When this initiation began, I was fortunate to already be in Daré, a community that is dedicated to healing and peacemaking. (Daré is open to all and meets once a month in East Oakland—more info at www.BayAreaDare.com.) From day one, that community stood by me listening and responding to calls from many sources.

Elenna was a key person and helped me so much to understand this journey in a different way than would have been my normal inclination. She kept seeing and sharing with me the wider picture she saw.

In her letter marking the one-month anniversary of the surgery, Elenna said, "...Thank you for allowing, no trusting me, to accompany you on this journey. It has been such a privilege to be washed in your tears, stretched and enlightened by your questions, collapsed in the laughter of true surrender, and warmed by the feel of you moment by moment more fully inhabiting the blessing of your wisdom body...."

I understand now important it is for people to be included in meaningful ways in something that I once might have thought of as a private matter. Being open to accompaniment on this journey was not just for me.

I was merely a vehicle for the kind of healing that took place for all of us.

And still... and still I thank you for accompanying me in rituals, in wisdom circles, in healing circles, in waiting rooms, in exam rooms. Thank you for your prayers, your listening, your wisdom, your gifts, your poetry, your bodywork and oils, your nurturance, your steadfastness and for changing everything about where and how we traveled.

Because of the responses I received during this time, I feel that a record of this journey could be useful in helping others through similar experiences and for all of us who run into what appear to be obstacles. I am working on a chap book that will contain my e-mails to you and many of the responses that you sent me. If there is personal material in your responses to me and you want to be sure I do not include it, please let me know. Also, I will look for anything that someone may not want to share and ask you about it. I will send out a final draft to this list and you can check it to be sure you are comfortable with what you said to me being printed.

If there were just one thing to say about this past five months, it would be that to flourish, we need community; community needs us; and our world needs us in extended communities that include much more than just humans. If you haven't got such a community, please find one or go out and create one of your own.

Stay Spacious and Be Well,
Elise

∂⁰

Due to technical difficulties, I lost the responses to that last e-mail. I remember feeling a bit at a loss knowing that I would not be sending out any more messages. But I felt the e-mails had taken me as far as I needed to go.

Now I was on my own.

In December, I published *Strands*[2] As soon as it was published, I was able to get my right arm out of the water when I swam for the first time since April.

TOES IN THE WATERS OF ACCEPTANCE

I continued to swim at the Y with a prosthesis in my bathing suit. I was able to shower and change without too much psychic effort, though I noticed that for a long while

---

2   See www.ArtBetweenUs.org.

it did take extra energy to manage. At some point I made a rule for myself that if the enclosed showers near the wall were ever both taken when I needed them, I would shower out in the open. I had to do this several times, and while there was some charge for me around it, I did it anyway.

One time a woman who had had a mastectomy came in beside me to my left and seemed unconcerned about hiding. It was the first time that I saw such a thing at the Y except for the time Karen came with me. Though I didn't speak to her, that woman gave me courage.

One day in February, I got to the Y and I realized that I had forgotten the prosthetic breast. I was with my swimming buddy Peggy and wanted her to be a kind of shield for me, to stand on that side of me so she would block any stares. But each time I needed her to do that, she was otherwise engaged, and I was forced to do it on my own. It was probably better that way since then I felt stronger when all was said and done. The following letter tells more details.

∂

February 12
Dear ones,

I am writing to those of you who were particularly involved in my returning to swimming after the surgery because there has been a development.

This past week, on the morning of my father's birthday (He has been dead for twelve years), I put fresh flowers on the ancestor altar for him and sang him Happy Birthday. Later that day, I found myself at the Y without my prosthesis (I forgot it). I debated for less than a minute about what to do. I dressed without it and went swimming and into the hot tub as well.

*When I got in, I felt the water surrounding my true bound-
aries, not the fake one I had been dragging in there with me, I felt
stronger than I have since I fell last April. And I felt freer and stronger
in spirit than I have ever felt... My father was there with me (he had
both feet amputated and swam anyway when he could, amidst the
stares, and became an expert on throwing self-consciousness to the
wind). I swam so strong and true. In the hot tub later, I saw some
stares, but I wondered to myself if I had been wearing the prosthesis
for them, or for me. If it was for me, I didn't need it any longer and if
it was for them, well, I thought, they can just deal with it themselves.*

*In Oregon last July I remember thinking "who do I have to
become to make this thing okay?" I wrote a poem and the first lines
were:*

> *When I lose a breast*
> *what will counterbalance it?*
> *What needs to grow bigger, more spacious*
> *to bear disfigurement,*
> *to balance asymmetry?*
> *A stronger heart, perhaps,*
> *a spirit short on self-consciousness*
> *A spirit who does not lean forward*
> *precariously into a future wicked with trouble,*
> *but one who sees beyond face value*
> *and screams,*
> *"YES, I know what I love."*

> *It is here. It is now.*

*Thanks to all of you for your support, for this did not happen
to me alone.*

> *Love,*
> *Elise*

ॐ

BOOK RELEASE PARTY

In March I had a book release party for my novel *Strands* at the Home of Truth in Alameda. Owlsnake, Elenna, and I planned it and brought in Beth, Lucinda, and Kaaren from the Sound Healing class to help call in the directions.

It was set up as an on-stage conversation with three chairs: one for OwlSnake, one for me, and one for my grandmother (complete with jacket, hat and shoes). It was a three-way discussion of the process of writing the book which, of course, involved the breast cancer as well.

Before the event, I somehow intuited the message from my grandmother that I was not to wear the prosthesis, so I went without it for the first time in public (aside from the pool). My grandmother didn't believe in cutting off parts of herself to conform to some cultural norm (so I assume adding parts for that same reason wouldn't pass muster with her). She never seemed to have the option to pass for something she wasn't; it felt important that I not pass either. She had been a strident feminist before it was fashionable, and she never stayed silent in the face of oppression. As I mentioned, that stridence caused her to be institutionalized for much of her life.

The event was a great success, with attendance and participation by people from the four corners of my life. We had people write names of their ancestors on pieces of paper and place them at one of the four altars in the room representing the four directions. The place was alive with the presences of those alive, and those who were gone but not forgotten.

That night I felt very close to my grandmother and

proud of myself for finishing and publishing the story that perhaps would let her rest in peace.

Each time I did a reading, my shoulder got a little better, until I read at the Berkeley Public Library, the last in the scheduled series of readings. After that, I declared the shoulder healed, and assumed that my grandmother had been able to move on.

GRADUATION FROM SOUND HEALING CLASS

In June I graduated from the Sound Healing class, one of the best things I have ever done in my life. I recommend it to everyone.

In that class, I met Kaaren with whom I became a business partner in a company called Heart Passages. We collaborate with people and Spirit to create eclectic inclusive ceremonies and rituals to mark life passages.

We had a month or so to come up with a final project and, sometime during that month, I woke up in the middle of the night and wrote my personal initiation story in relation to sound healing. I knew I was being asked to present it to the class. I had told my story to maybe a third of my classmates and the others would hear it then for the first time. Making it public in that way, even just to the class, was a challenge for me,

Kaaren, Tina and I decided that for our final project, I would present my story, "The Power of Ritual," which would lead directly into a ritual for the class to mark our graduation. We asked that people bring something precious to them that they could give away, and at the beginning of the ritual, we asked that they put the gifts in the baskets chanting, "**As I let go, so I open.**"

At the end of the ritual, each person drew a gift out of the basket. Their intentions for going forward were put in a brass bowl and rung into the world and later burned on the beach, making sure that they were released into the world. The following is the graduation story I presented to the class:

June 13
The Power of Ritual

I had many other choices to use as my presentation but it kept coming to me that my story is one that we all need to hear to step into the field we have trained for.

I started this class at a different point in my life from most of you. For me, the really hard stuff, at least for this particular phase of my story, was over. The loss, the initiation, had already happened and I was in neutral gear, as John Beaulieu[3] would say. A few days after I decided to enroll in this class, I discovered a huge lump in my breast and just one week before class started, I had a mastectomy. I recall the dread I felt when the first class was moved up a week and I realized how quickly I was being asked to step back into the flow of my life.

That Saturday class was my first public appearance since the surgery. I brought an escort because I wasn't driving yet, and I truly had no idea if I could make it through the class physically, let alone emotionally. I had written an e-mail to Silvia,[4] but as we all found out later, she doesn't read long e-mails. So I had no allies, no one to watch out for me. I left the class at about 2:30 p.m. because of physical tiredness but I had done okay with the emotional part.

After that the allies showed themselves rapidly. I told my story in

3   John Beaulieu was a favorite teacher of mine in the sound healing class. In his cosmology, loss creates space (neutral gear) and allows one to shift into any one of the elements (earth, air, fire or water) as needed for balance and euphoria. See www.biosonics.com.

4   Silvia Nakkach, Director of the Sound, Voice and Music Healing Certificate program: www.voxmundiproject.com

the first small group we had that included Debbie and Kaaren. It helped so much to have somebody there who knew what I was going through. And as it turned out, I was ready for the class. I didn't need extra assistance. I had so much space just then from the loss I had suffered.

Maybe some of you noticed the cover on my notebook for class has a picture of a plaster cast of my torso that was made with the help of good friends a few days before surgery. I put it there to make sure I would be constantly reminded to stay awake, not to return to normal. I remember John saying, "Being 'normal' keeps us from adapting." The picture on my notebook helped me to stay awake, kept me from returning to normal.

I was particularly taken with Beaulieu's way of seeing the world—it explained to me how I could have suffered such a loss and felt happier than I ever have. I'll repeat that—when I started this class one week after surgery, I was happier than I have ever been. This trauma had been an opportunity for adaptation and shift of consciousness.

But to back up a bit, I want to offer how this came to be for me, to share with you the possibilities of sound healing and of community. Because I did not come to that place alone. I had a community, a healing circle that I have been with for eight years called Daré, a Shona word for "Council." From the day after I discovered the lump in my breast to now, I have had people around me who could ground this experience in the Spiritual realm and take it from one of horror to a connectedness with all beings.

Soon after I discovered the lump, I began referring to it as a stranger who had come to town—I just needed to determine why he had shown up so that I could politely ask him to leave. That part wasn't so easy. I had to work through the fear and anger at his sudden appearance. I couldn't look at him, let alone speak politely to him. We had two music Daré's for me—picture what we did the second time John Beaulieu came—collaborative healing with music and touch and Spirit. The second healing session was mainly people to whom I had taught didgeridoo, playing for me—six didges around me. The community kept reminding me to see the spiritual meanings in each step of the journey. That proved to be indispensable.

At first, of course, we worked to get rid of the tumor, or at least shrink it, trying to move the stranger gently on out of town, but as it turned out, that was not what healing was to look like for me. He did not go away voluntarily, even with so many prayers and so much music. In fact, he threat-ened to kill me if I let him stay. He was so stubbornly rooted there that the only way to be sure the threat was gone was to remove the whole breast.

To add insult, for other reasons I won't go into, I could not have a reconstruction of the breast. I was to be marked forever. There was no going back to normal.

There are many twists and turns and beautifully choreographed lessons from the universe in the story that I can't go into now because of time, but I am writing a book called, "When Things Happen to People: The Field Beyond Good and Bad" where I will tell the rest.

I want to finish by telling you about a ritual I had the day before surgery, which was how I came to believe so deeply in the power of ritual, and to readily accept Kaaren's offer to become a partner in Heart Passages, whose business it is to collaborate with people and Spirit to create rituals.

It was suggested to me that maybe I needed a ritual prior to surgery. I cringed, not knowing how to begin something like that. I pictured myself walking out somewhere at dawn all by myself in prayer and thought maybe I could do that; at first, I couldn't even imagine asking others to join me. But the "how" of ritual kept being revealed to me. I first knew it had to be at dawn, facing East. Then I got that it should be on the Inspiration Point Trail in Tilden at the point where you can see both Mt. Tamalpais and Mt. Diablo. For this ritual, it seemed I needed to have mostly men. I went so far as to ask four men and they all quickly agreed to meet me there at dawn on September 3, the day before my surgery. I still didn't know what I was going to do with them.

At some point (and these revelations usually came to me in conversation with my Daré friends), I realized that the ritual was going to be a kind of wedding and the men were there to give me away. I had guidance that I had done enough mourning and I was to celebrate. That was inconceivable to me, but I thought I would try it, at least go through the motions.

The men gathered around me in the dawning moments of that day and we faced the rising sun over the right shoulder of Mt. Diablo. I was dressed in white. They lowered me face down on the earth and I entrained[5]

5   "Entrain" in a word used in sound healing to mean to tune into an other being and sing, play an instrument, or just breathe in time with the other's breath or rhythm.

my breath with that of the earth. Then I got up on my knees and made my vows, giving my breast as a token of my love for the nurturance of All of Our Relations, that I would forever remember my place in the web of life. They left me alone then as I prayed and played didge to the rising sun.

Going into the ritual I had no idea what might happen. I heavily doubted that I could believe I was voluntarily giving my breast as an offering. How could that be possible? But the ritual with music, with nature and with Spirit conspired, and I watched myself wake up to this reframing of the moment. My consciousness was transformed. Nothing was being taken away from me; I was offering a gift of gratitude for this shift of consciousness.

I needed community to constantly remind me of music and sound and to stand by me when I needed witnesses and co-hearts. If you get nothing else out of this story, let it be that you find a community in which you have people who will be this for you, in the hard times and in the day-to-day times, either from this co-heart or from one you develop or find. Daré is open to anyone and meets once a month; I am happy to talk to you about it if you are interested.

So I say to you now as we prepare for the ritual that Tina, Kaaren and I will lead, that if your intention is full of integrity, this ritual will be full of power. Your consciousness has the potential, at all times, to shift into neutral and be guided into higher states. And sometimes it just needs a little help from your friends. Initiation is not something we go through only once. We are initiated many times throughout our lives. It is up to us to recognize the initiation and be thankful for the chance to give up something dear to us to create the space for the alchemic change into higher states of consciousness, from 'normal' into euphoric light beings.

The gifts we brought to the altar today represent the giving up, the initiation, the loss. Let us create spaciousness with our music and our hearts. Let us be the healing presence we want to see in this world. And let us start now as we pick up our instruments and gifts and line up into two lines facing each other…

ও

The response from our classmates was passionate, with many claiming that our ritual was their spiritual graduation.

SPIRIT BREAST

Some time later, but before the one-year anniversary of the surgery, I began feeling that I couldn't wear the prosthesis when I was participating in healings at Daré. I felt that my vanity actually blocked healing energy.

I began to feel, not as if I was lacking something, but that I had actually gained what I am calling a spirit breast. It is almost as if my fleshly breast has been replaced by something that wants to be in contact with others (people, animals, plants, the land itself). So I have begun wearing the prosthesis very seldom, and never to Daré or when I participate in any kind of healing.

I have yet to fully comprehend it, but this entity makes itself known at strange times. It twitches, hurts, or itches at odd moments and reminds me to pay particular attention. It feels like a healing tool, a kind of diving rod that I am still in training to use well.

I decided to enjoy asymmetry as best I can, fashioning my clothes to fit my asymmetric body. I play with what asymmetry does to a life. Back when I was worrying about the surgery, I wrote this about asymmetry:

      ↎

Perfect balance is stasis—nothing can change.
A state in which there is neither motion
nor development
often results from opposing forces balancing each other.
When opposing forces suddenly do not balance,
there is a shift from stasis.
To movement.
To change.

❧

Almost exactly one year after I went through this surgery, another Daré woman was diagnosed with breast cancer. I walked through it with her in a way that would have been impossible if I had not gone through this myself. I was able to be compassionate but not pulled into all of the emotions of it. I could help her by staying with my own truth and walking beside her, not trying to take the pain away. I could feel in myself the growth of someone who can be of assistance in healing, one who has deep compassion, but who at the same time is not trying to rescue someone else.

Why is this Daré is having so many instances of breast cancer? I do not know. But I do know that the rate of breast cancer in the Bay Area is higher than in most other places for reasons that no one knows. I'm hoping someone figures that out soon.

Metaphorically, the breast has tentacles in so many places in this society: the obsession with the surface of female beauty; breast as a symbol of nurturance; breast as Mother, for better or for worse; the breast as our first understanding of our survival need for others. These places are deep and full of associations for each of us at different points in our lives.

I ask myself the question, "How can I be more nurturing, not just to human babies, but to all of our connections? How can the offering of this breast assist me in healing the breaches between us: between humans; between humans and all other beings; between humans and the land, the air, the oceans and rivers? Between humans and our ancestors? What can I do to further sustainability on this planet? These happen to be the very questions that the Daré community addresses.

So I Open

This story has no ending, so I decided to stop it when it spiraled itself back into itself. Remember, I was telling Elenna a dream when the ladder fell across the highway? The dream I was telling was this:

My sister and I are going to a conference of hers somewhere outside of the country. Before we register at the hotel, we go out to the beach. There, a hollow log has washed onshore and my sister picks it up and asks if I can play it. I try but there are four holes in it, and I can see the water bubbling out of those holes. I ask my sister to plug up the holes with her fingers, which she does, and then I can play it. It has a great sound and I want to take it home with me. We walk up to the hotel with it and run into a man who tells us that he has many logs, just like this one, at his house, that people give him because they are not allowed on the plane.

When we register, I try to find out where we are because I can't remember, and I see a map and on it Pelican Bay is circled.

In another dream I had had before I started using the didge for healing, *I am in Costa Rica and I am handed a spiral didgedridoo by a doctor and told to use it for healing.*

In June, my sister and I (in real life) were sitting under a temporary shelter from the bright sun at Steep Ravine beach, when she reached over and picked up a dried piece of bull whip kelp dried into a spiral shape. She handed it to me, asking if I could play it. We used a rock to create an opening on the bulb end. I then put it to my lips and immediately played a beautiful sound. She calls herself Oceana.

Oceana has become my partner in healing. People tell me her sound is sweet, her vibration gentle, penetrating and healing. When we give one-on-one didge hugs or healings, spirals of energy envelope all of us, creating a swirling healing field.

And so we spiral back to the telling of the dream and the ladder falling. Neither good nor bad, this ladder, but a reminder to us all to climb beyond a one-dimensional life, to dwell more fully in the healing field, alive in its myriad dimensions, seen and unseen, still and full of vibration, always and forever connected to each other and to all creation.

spirit breast

oceana appeared
to my sister on the shore
of pelican bay as we huddled
under shelter from solstice sun

thrusting this dried bull whip kelp
into my hands, she asked
can you play this

we opened the bulb   smoothed the edge
then yes I could play her
she whispered in our ears   came home with us
does not stop speaking

took her to daré   could hear her distinct voice
urging me to play her now without delay

before we called ourselves present to spirit
i asked if we could begin quietly
with only her sound

then her call vibrated forth   rallying
spirits of oceans   of humans   spirits
of ancestors   whales   dolphins

she sang to wind
to ocean floor's hemorrhage
to the struggling creatures
and to those who know

how to heal it

she called for peace
to the female in us all
to emerge into fresh air
out from under thickening gloom

smelling of the sea   she touches us
where our own sea meets the skin of us
dares us to bare our spirit breasts

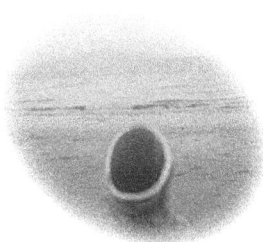

that we may suckle the world
back into alignment with life
the rolling sea   the breeze that wakes up
the swimmer in us

inviting us to listen to the repetitive pulse of
the world that we forget to dance to

that we first heard in the womb
no need for amplification
the vibration that made us come alive

made our hearts beat for the first time
oceana reminds us who we are
who our relatives are

who madly dances with us
who arouses the beat
more than a muse
music of breath

spirit breast

Order this Book:

To obtain a signed copy using Paypal, go to
www.ArtBetweenUs.org.

To order on-line with credit card, go to
https://www.createspace.com/3499309

S. Elise Peeples is:

Author of *Strands*, a novel based on four generations of women in her family; and ***The Emperor Has A Body: Body-Politics in the Between***, a critique of western philosophy and ethics and a vision for collaboration.

www.ArtBetweenUs.org

Founder of Sound Rivers, where she plays and teaches didgeridoo for healing purposes.

www.SoundRivers.net

Executive Director of Art Between Us, Inc., a non-profit corporation specializing in collaborative art.

www.ArtBetweenUs.org

Co-Director of Heart Passages which collaborates with people and Spirit to design eclectic rituals for life passages.

www.HeartPassages.com

www.ingramcontent.com/pod-product-compliance
Lightning Source LLC
Chambersburg PA
CBHW020909090426
42736CB00008B/546